Agriculture, poverty and reform in Iran

As in many developing countries, the prospects for land reform in Iran seemed promising. It was expected to improve rural poverty and stimulate agricultural development by replacing the traditional landlord-peasant system with more peasant-biased, modern farming.

This book assesses the economic consequences of land reform, focusing particularly on its effect on the living standards of the rural poor. Amid describes a 'bimodal' system of large and small farms that emerged after the reform. Large farms, with government support, modernized and grew more profitable cash crops, whereas smaller farms found difficulty in obtaining credit and continued to rely on traditional techniques and staple food crops. Unfortunately, he argues, land reform was not, contrary to official propaganda, a success for the majority of the Iranian rural population, who experienced virtually no improvement in living standards and a growth of rural inequality as a result.

Mohammad Javad Amid is a Lecturer in Economics at the University of Uppsala.

Agriculture, poverty and reform in Iran

Mohammad Javad Amid

London and New York

First published 1990 by Routledge
11 New Fetter Lane, London EC4P 4EE

Simultaneously published in the USA and Canada
by Routledge
a division of Routledge, Chapman and Hall, Inc.
29 West 35th Street, New York, NY 10001

© 1990 Mohammad Javad Amid

Typeset by Pat and Anne Murphy, Highcliffe-on-Sea, Dorset
Printed and bound in Great Britain by
Mackays of Chatham PLC, Chatham, Kent

British Library Cataloguing in Publication Data

Amid, Mohammad Javad, *1949–*
  Agriculture, poverty and reform in Iran.
  1. Iran. Agricultural land. Land tenure. Reform
  I. Title
  333.3350955

  ISBN 0-415-03561-9

Library of Congress Cataloging-in-Publication Data

applied for
ᵀᴾ

Contents

Contents

Figures

Tables

Acknowledgements

I began to write this book as my doctoral dissertation at Uppsala University, Sweden. Since its completion less than two years ago, I have received comments and suggestions and thought over certain sections. My subsequent revision of the dissertation has now resulted in this book.

I have benefited considerably from others in completing this study. I wish to acknowledge my great debts to Professor Mats Lundahl who provided me with his kind and encouraging supervision. His thorough readings of various drafts of the study and suggestions for the improvement of both form and content were extremely valuable. I am also heavily indebted to Olle Mellander, who read and commented on almost everything I wrote concerning this study and was kindly ready to advise me at any time.

I would like to express my gratitude to Professor Göran Ohlin who provided me with helpful supervision in the early stages of my research. Thanks are also due to Yngve Andersson, Christer Gunnarsson, Professor Fred Halliday, Rojelio Imable, Keith McLachlan, Christian Nilsson, Cyrus Salmanzadeh, Chris Scott and Bo Utas whose suggestions, encouragement and help at different stages of my study were of great importance. Moreover, my thanks go to the participants of the seminars at the Department of Economics, Lund University, where various chapters of this study were discussed.

I am also deeply indebted to Professor Ann K.S. Lambton who kindly read almost all of the chapters concerning Iran. Her valuable comments substantially improved this work. Furthermore, I owe a great debt to Professor Bo Gustafsson for his useful comments and encouragement and to Professor Bengt-Christer Ysander for stimulating me to speed up the completion of this research during its final stages, when it was really required.

Special thanks are also due to Alan Harkess for correcting and polishing my English and to Eva Holst, who very kindly and skilfully typed many versions of this study. Moreover, I am very grateful to Jan Wallanders Stiftelse whose generous grants contributed much to the accomplishment of my research.

Last but not least, I have to express my deep appreciation to my wife and our daughter for their patience in putting up with my long preoccupation with working on this book.

Uppsala
M.J. Amid

Administrative division of Iran, 1966

Chapter one

Introduction

Iran, like many other developing countries, has experienced a land reform in recent decades. The Iranian land reform programme started in early 1962 accompanied by considerable rhetoric. Speeches and statements made by various government authorities gave the impression that eroding rural poverty and stimulating agricultural development were among the major objectives of the programme. The reform was also initiated without delay. The complete implementation of the land reform programme, however, lasted about a decade and went through three different stages during this period.

A relatively large number of Iranian peasants have received land as a result of the land reform and the application of modern inputs, such as fertilizers and tractors, increased substantially in farming after the reform. On the whole, a new agrarian system replaced the traditional landlord—peasant system which was believed to have hampered agricultural and rural development. Nevertheless, the agricultural growth rate did not rise markedly and there was hardly any improvement in the standard of living of the majority of the peasantry.

There is no doubt that many political, social, and economic factors contributed to bring about the prevailing situation in rural Iran. There are also many valuable studies which discuss various aspects of the Iranian land reform. However, most of the literature, especially the books, focuses on socio-political aspects of the land reform programme. The major purpose of the present study is to provide a detailed economic analysis of the reform and its economic consequences. The emphasis, however, will be on the effects of the reform upon the levels of living of the rural poor.

The pattern of the study

The study is divided into eight chapters. Chapter 1 is the introduction, which also contains some general information on Iranian agriculture. Chapters 2 and 3 are devoted to the analysis of traditional tenancy systems in general and the Iranian pre-reform agrarian system in particular. This will pave the way for understanding why agrarian changes are believed to be necessary in such systems and how land reform, which is a widely recommended means for such changes, can affect the prevailing conditions in these systems. The latter issue is discussed at length in Chapter 4 and will be followed by a study of the Iranian land reform in Chapters 5 to 8. Let us look at each chapter more closely.

Since the traditional agrarian system in Iran was a tenancy system, Chapter 2 begins the study with a general discussion of agricultural backwardness in traditional tenancy systems. We examine the major features of such systems which are often alleged to hinder agricultural progress and cause rural poverty. The emphasis of the discussion, however, will be on the theory of sharecropping because (a) sharecropping was the dominant form of land tenure in Iranian agriculture before the reform; and (b) the system was widely believed to have certain shortcomings that were detrimental to agricultural development.

In the light of the theoretical analysis of Chapter 2, Chapter 3 explores the traditional agrarian system in Iran. We want to see whether the system retarded agricultural development and contributed to the impoverishment and indebtedness of most of the rural people. The arguments for changing traditional agrarian systems are mainly based on the presence of such problems in these systems.

Chapter 4 will turn to the theory of land reform. Land reform is often suggested as a means to bring about desirable agrarian changes in many developing countries. The major aim of this chapter is to explain in detail how land reform may, or may not, succeed in improving the lot of the peasantry and stimulating agricultural progress. We argue that the ultimate results of a land redistribution programme depend highly on whether the programme alters a traditional tenancy system into a 'bimodal' or a 'unimodal' system. The former comprises principally very small and very large farmers while the latter consists of small family farms. We maintain that it is the unimodal agrarian system which can raise the levels of living of the majority of the rural people.

Chapter 5 introduces the basic features of the Iranian land reform programme. We will examine the laws and regulations of the reform to see whether they aimed at a unimodal or a bimodal agrarian system. This will be followed by Chapter 6 which studies the actual impact of the reform programme on the agrarian system in Iran. To begin with, Chapter 6 traces the implementation of the land reform laws in order to estimate the amount of land that was redistributed and the proportion of the rural population who received land. This chapter will then try to identify the major characteristics of the post-reform Iranian agrarian system.

Having followed the formation of a new agrarian system in Iran as a result of the land reform, we will study the economic consequences of the change in the agrarian system in Chapter 7. We intend to examine post-reform Iranian agriculture to find out, for instance, whether the majority of farmers could modernize their methods of cultivation and improve their production after the land reform. The importance of these changes for the well-being of the majority of the rural population will be discussed in Chapter 8. This chapter concludes the study by examining the living conditions of the rural people in the 1970s to see whether or not they experienced any marked improvement after the land reform.

Difficulties concerning the statistics

It is appropriate here perhaps to examine some of the shortcomings concerning the data although we will refer to such problems repeatedly throughout the study. To begin with, we should point out that our empirical analyses are principally based on official statistics.[1] These statistics, which have been released by various ministries and governmental organizations, are notoriously unreliable and often inconsistent. For instance, there are sometimes considerable discrepancies between the two main sources of agricultural data, namely the Ministry of Agriculture and the Statistical Centre of Iran. As a matter of fact, the former frequently reported higher production figures for almost all types of crops (see Table 7.11, p. 127). On the whole, the agricultural data of the Statistical Centre are often believed to be more reliable.[2]

One major source of the unreliability of the official statistics might have been the officials' anxiety to give a favourable impression of the prevailing situation. There is also sporadic evidence which confirms such a belief. For example, when the consumption inquiries of the Central Bank indicated the deterioration of food consumption between 1959 and 1966, the Central Bank maintained that such a result 'did not appear to be plausible'. Therefore, the higher consumption figures of 1959 were brought down to the level of the 1966 figures (see Bank Markazi Iran 1969: 106–7 and Brun and Dumont 1978: 16). It is then reasonable to believe that the official statistics generally exaggerate the successes and underestimate the failures.

Lack of statistics is another problem. For example, there is little information available about the amount of land which was distributed among the peasants under the land reform programme. In such cases, one has to rely on the estimates made by others or try to make one's own estimates on reasonable grounds.

We treat, therefore, the official statistics critically and attempt to give a more realistic picture by using other available information. We are also cautious about our conclusions and compare them with the findings of other Iranian rural studies, especially the field research if available. Consequently, we believe that the major conclusions of the study broadly reflect the reality.

Iranian agriculture: a general view

Like most of the developing countries, Iran was predominantly an agricultural country in the early 1960s. The agricultural sector, which consists of farming, animal husbandry, forestry and fishing, employed more than 50 per cent of the labour force and produced about one-third of GNP at that time (Statistical Centre of Iran 1966: 88; Bank Markazi Iran 1974: 32–3). On the whole, over 65 per cent of the population lived in the rural areas and must have relied mainly on agriculture for their living.

However, the significance of agriculture has been decreasing in recent decades. In 1976, only 34 per cent of labour force was engaged in agriculture and produced less than 10 per cent of GNP (Statistical Centre of Iran 1984: 65; Bank Markazi Iran, *Annual Report and Balance Sheet* 1977: 10; for further information about changes in the Iranian economy in this period see MacLachlan 1977). The rural population also decreased to 53 per cent of the total by 1976 (Statistical Centre of Iran 1984: 42).

Rural people principally live and work in about 60,000 villages.[3] These villages differ from each other in many respects. Some of them have several hundred families while some others consist of a few farmsteads with only a handful of families.[4] Some are located in more fertile areas and the villagers are prosperous; others are located in less fertile areas and the villagers have more difficulties in achieving a bare subsistence.

The prosperity of the Iranian villagers is generally determined by the availability of water for farming. Generally speaking, it is due to the shortage of water that only one-tenth of the total area of the country is cultivable (see Table 1.1).

Table 1.1 Land utilization in Iran, 1977 (thousand hectares)

Total area of the country		165,000
Total arable land		15,400
Rain-fed arable land:		
Under cultivation	5,600	
Fallow	4,200	
Irrigated arable land:		
Under cultivation	3,600	
Fallow	2,000	

Source: Statistical Centre of Iran (1984: 335)

The average rainfall for the country is roughly 300 mm per annum, i.e. it is only one-third of the average annual rainfall for the world. As Figure 1.1. shows, there are also great regional variations in average annual precipitation. For example, most of the central, southern and south-eastern regions receive between 100 and 200 mm of rainfall a year while the average precipitation in parts of the Caspian littoral is from 1,500 to 2,000 mm (for further information see Aresvik 1976: 1–9).

If we consider the fact that the rain-fed farming requires at least 250 mm of rain, Figure 1.2 illustrates that such farming is possible mainly in certain areas of Iran. As a result, rain-fed agriculture is generally practised in those provinces which lie in these regions, i.e. Gilan, Mazandaran, Azarbayjan, Kordestan, Kermanshah, and parts of Khorasan, Fars and Khuzestan (see further Aresvik 1976; Taqavi 1983). In the other areas, agriculture is largely dependent on irrigation water. As Table 1.1 indicates, the lands which are culti-vated with the help of irrigation water constitute more than one-third of the total arable land.

Irrigation water is provided by underground channels (*qanats*), wells, dams, rivers, and springs. Until recently, *qanats* were by far the most important source of irrigation in Iran. By 1960, more than 75 per cent of all water used for irrigation came from these under-ground channels (Wulff 1966: 251).

The *qanat* system shows how skilfully Iranian peasants have tried to cope with water shortages. *Qanats* were dug to collect under-ground water and bring it to the surface. The construction of a *qanat* requires a great deal of experience and skill. The *qanat* builder has to determine first where a *qanat* system could be dug considering the natural conditions and the estimated flow of water. A head well is sunk into the water-bearing layer, above the land to be irrigated. A sloping conduit is then dug, the gradient of which is

5

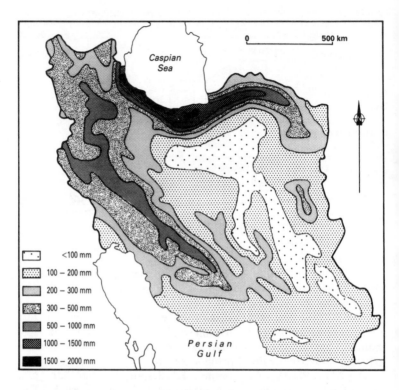

Figure 1.1 Annual precipitation in Iran
Source: Aresvik (1976: 4)

such that the water is able to flow along it under the influence of gravity and so reach the surface. Wells are dug at intervals along the length of the *qanat* to provide fresh air for the diggers and through which the soil can be brought to the surface and emptied. (For more information about *qanat* construction see Wulff 1966: 251–4.) Figure 1.2 illustrates a sectional view of a *qanat*.

The depth of a *qanat*, its length and the amount of water it provides depends on the local conditions. The depth of a head well could be between 20 to 90 m while the length of a *qanat* could be up to 70 km. A *qanat* may irrigate only a few hectares or more than one village (Lambton 1953: 217–20; Khosrovi 1979a: 97). The numbers given for *qanats* vary greatly. It is estimated that they might have numbered about 50,000, with an average length of 5 km; i.e. an underground channel of 250,000 km (Khirabi 1981:

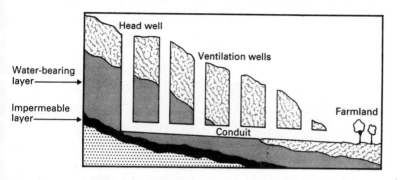

Figure 1.2 Sectional view of a *qanat*
Source: Wulff (1966: 249)

56). The first official statistics in 1954 estimated that there were about 21,000 *qanats*, 8,500 of them out of use (Taqavi 1983: 71). A large number of *qanats* lie in the central, eastern and south-eastern regions, i.e. the less rainy areas (Taqavi 1983: 69).

Springs and wells were also main sources of irrigation water, next in importance to *qanats*. Usually, a channel dug on the soil surface led such water to farms. Spring water was sometimes conducted into the *qanats* rather than being used directly (Adabi 1955: 157). There were also special *qanats* which were dug only to bring the river water to farms. These *qanats* were constructed where the configuration of the surface prevented farmers from using ordinary channels (Wulff 1966: 152).

Since there are high climatic differences from region to region, cultivating periods vary in different regions. For example, wheat is harvested during March and April in the Khuzestan plains while it is harvested from July to September in the mountain regions (Aresvik 1976: 73). During the winter, which is the most rainy period, lands are normally allocated to wheat and barely in most parts of the country. These are the principle staple crops in Iran, except in Gilan and Mazandaran in the Caspian littoral, where rice is the major staple crop. In 1960, more than 76 per cent of the cultivated land was under wheat and barley (Agah Book Collection 1982: 181). Some land is also cultivated during the summer. Summer crops consist mainly of vegetables and fruits such as cucumber and melon in many parts of the country.

Chapter two

Agricultural backwardness in theory

Development studies generally consider traditional agrarian systems as an impediment to agricultural progress and rural development in Third World countries. They argue that traditional institutions in these countries are principally responsible for low productivity, widespread unemployment and underemployment, low investments, and uneven distribution of income in rural areas. The traditional agrarian system in Iran, known as the landlord–peasant system, was often criticized on similar grounds.

The Iranian landlord–peasant system was in fact a traditional tenancy system. That is to say, most of land ownership was concentrated in a few hands but cultivated by tenants in the form of small farms. Moreover, a large majority of the Iranian tenants were sharecroppers which meant that they paid a share of the crop to the landlords for farming the land.

Studying the essence of the above arguments in the context of such systems is important for understanding agricultural and rural development strategies. Thus, the present chapter is devoted to the major problems of traditional agrarian systems in developing countries focusing on the issues which are relevant to the Iranian landlord–peasant system.

We begin the discussion by examining the main features and problems of traditional tenancy systems and we will then turn to the sharecropping debate. Sharecropping was not only a prominent feature of the Iranian agrarian system but also a tenure system which was widely attacked as being defective. There was a general consensus that sharecropping reduced peasants' labour input and deprived them of the incentive to invest in land. In view of the dominance of sharecropping in Iran and its importance in land reform discussion, we will study the theory of sharecropping in some detail.

Traditional tenancy systems: major features and problems

Traditional tenancy systems, or landlord–peasant systems, are the dominant type of agrarian systems in many countries in Asia and the Middle East.[1] Land ownership is concentrated in the hands of a few landlords, but in spite of the high degree of land concentration, land is usually cultivated in the form of smallholdings. In other words, landlords divide their land into small farms and lease them to farmers. The tenants cultivate the farms and pay rent. The rent can be a share of the crop (sharecropping) or a fixed amount per unit of land, in kind or cash.

A great number of landowners live in cities and often have other economic activities there. These absentee landowners administer their landed property through salaried agents. Agriculture as such may be of secondary importance for these landlords. They hold the land not only for income but also for social status and political power. Rent collection may be their only function in agriculture. Sometimes they may also provide consumption credits, construct and repair irrigation systems, etc. (Warriner 1969: 46).

A high degree of land concentration is a key issue in most criticisms of traditional tenancy systems. First and foremost, land concentration results in a highly skewed distribution of income in the agricultural sector. This in turn may adversely affect agricultural progress when it is combined with absenteeism. In fact, absentee landlordism is often singled out as a factor which deprives agriculture of its potential investment resources.

Large landowners normally transfer most of their agriculture income to the cities to finance their consumption and other activities there. In fact, high propensities to consume (an alleged feature of large landlords), in combination with the higher profitability of their urban financial and commercial activities, limit the investment capacity of the rent collected in agriculture.[2]

The tenants would probably not invest in land either. In the first place, a large majority of them are very poor and have nothing to invest. Second, they may have little incentive to invest in the tenanted farms since they lack security of tenancy. As a matter of fact, the tenants can be evicted at will.

It is reasonable to believe that insecurity of tenancy impedes investment in land by tenants. Even a quick-yielding investment, such as fertilizers, needs more than one crop year to bear its full fruits but tenants do not usually know whether their tenancy will last long enough to reap the returns of such investments. In fact, there is always the risk of being evicted the following year without any compensation for investment costs. A tenant is hardly ready to

9

invest in such insecure circumstances. Moreover, an improvement or innovation adopted by a tenant may promise a higher return and increase the value of his holding which might result in the transfer of the lease to another tenant willing to pay higher rent (Lundahl 1979: 603–5). Such a risk will naturally reinforce the tenant's hesitation to invest in his holding. There is perhaps an additional risk of eviction in the case of sharecropping: a landowner will gladly demand his share of an increased output which results from a tenant's improvement practices, but it seems doubtful that he would extend the contract with an unsuccessful innovative tenant.[3]

The above discussion indicates that part of the problem in the tenancy system stems from imperfectly defined property rights which do not guarantee that an individual will reap the benefits of his activities.

The risk of innovation is another factor which can deprive poor tenants of investment. Using new methods and seeds involves many more risks than the old ones since they are new and there is no previous experience upon which to predict the outcome. In addition, new seeds, fertilizers, and farming systems may all increase the variability of the harvest, i.e. increase the fluctuations around the average. On the other hand, the traditional methods do not promise high production but present low variance. The old technologies used over the generations have proved to guarantee their survival. Poor peasants are very likely to prefer, and get stuck with, traditional methods since these methods provide a better security for their survival.[4]

In sum, both landlords and tenants are reluctant to invest in agriculture in a traditional landlord–tenant system. This will hinder any technological change and innovation in agriculture and limits agricultural growth considerably. As a consequence, there might be further impoverishment of rural people as their number increases in the course of time.

Apart from the above criticisms that are directed toward the tenancy system as a whole, sharecropping, as a special kind of tenancy, has been widely perceived to have its own defects. The argument that sharecropping induces sharecroppers to undersupply variable inputs, discourages them to invest in land, and reduces output is perhaps as old as economics itself.[5] In fact, demands for the reform of sharecropping systems have been largely based on the premise that sharecropping is inefficient and causes underutilization of land and labour. This is, however, a controversial issue today, and in view of the importance of sharecropping in pre-reform Iran we will examine it in more detail.

Sharecropping and efficiency

The conventional wisdom, notably Marshall, argues that a share-cropper has an incentive to apply variable inputs less intensively than an owner-operator or a fixed-rent tenant (Marshall 1920: 534–7). Sharing violates the equality of marginal products of the same input in alternative uses and leads to a Pareto-inefficient allocation of resources. Let us look at this argument in detail.

Suppose that a crop with output Q is produced with land of area H and a labour force of L; i.e. $Q = F(H,L)$. Two farmers, an owner-operator and a sharecropper, cultivate holdings of the same size and fertility in a perfectly competitive and certain world. Further, assume that the sharecropper pays a fixed proportion, r, of gross output to the landlord and that r is traditionally determined.

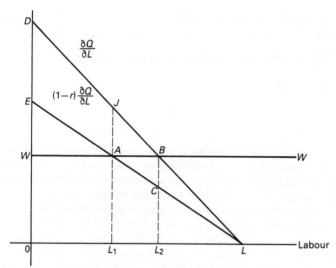

Figure 2.1 Determination of labour intensity in sharecropped and non-sharecropped lands: the traditional approach

In Figure 2.1 $\partial Q/\partial L$ represents the marginal productivity of labour in both farms. This is equal to the marginal income of the owner-operator, but the sharecropper receives only a percentage of this amount. Consequently, his marginal revenue is $(1-r)\partial Q/\partial L$. In terms of Figure 2.1, the sharecropper pays $DE/D0 = r$ of the crop to the landlord and keeps $E0/D0 = (1-r)$ of it for himself. The marginal cost of cultivation for both farmers is equal and constant at the market wage rate, W. To maximize revenue, each farmer equates his marginal revenue and cost which means that the owner-operator, or a fixed-tenant, uses L_2 of labour and produces $0DBL_2$ while the sharecropper employs only L_1 of labour and produces $0DJL_1$.[6] The marginal product of labour for sharecroppers is greater than his marginal cost by AJ, and the situation is not Pareto-optimal. The area AJB represents an economic loss which is imposed on the society by this tenure system.

The above approach leads to a surprising conclusion: in equilibrium, the marginal product of sharecropping land is equal to zero if the sharecropper is free to decide not only his labour input but also his land input. In fact, if the tenant is allowed, he determines the amount of his labour and the land he rents so that his income, y^t, is maximized. With the above mentioned assumptions, it means that we have:

$$\text{Max } y^t = (1-r)F(H,L) - WL \qquad (1)$$
$$(L,H)$$

and the necessary conditions for maximization are

$$(1-r)F_L = W \qquad (2)$$

$$F_H = 0 \qquad (3)$$

Equation (3) implies that tenants tend to rent more and more land until the value of the marginal product of land becomes zero.[7] Before this point, they can combine additional land with the same amount of labour and increase the output; they receive $(1-r)$ of the extra output without any extra cost for themselves.

Gale Johnson who was the first to note this implication of the traditional analysis, cast doubt upon its validity (Johnson 1950). It is hardly believable, he argues, that landlords allow tenants to cultivate the land so extensively. He suggests that landlords can force their tenants to cultivate the land intensively by undertaking one, or a mixture, of the following practices: (1) to specify in detail what the tenant is required to do; (2) to share in the costs in the same proportion as output is shared; and (3) to grant only short-term leases and check periodically the tenants' performance (Johnson 1950: 118).[8] However reluctant to accept the implication of inefficiency argument, Johnson does not provide an alternative explanation of sharecropping.[9]

Cheung was the first who formulated a simple general equilibrium model and arrived at the conclusion that resource allocation under sharecropping was efficient (Cheung 1968, 1969). Cheung's model is based on the crucial assumption that every landlord stipulates the tenant's labour intensity in the contract and is able to enforce such a provision. Under such circumstances, the landlord determines the sharecropper's labour input and the rental share so that he can maximize his income and the tenant receives a share equal to his alternative wage earning. The landlord's maximum income will accordingly be equal to what he could gain if he either cultivated the land himself or rented it at a fixed rate. Cheung concludes that the landlord will stipulate the minimum labour input of the share-cropper at L_2, in terms of Figure 2.1, and thus the inefficiency noted in the traditional argument is eliminated.[10]

The landlord's behaviour in Cheung's model has raised many criticisms. Bardhan and Srinivasan criticize Cheung because he allows only the landlord to maximize his income and, moreover, to determine the rental share as a monopolist.[11] Another problem with Cheung's model is the way he treats the sharecropper. The share-cropper is required to deliver a certain amount of labour for a wage-equivalent income and thus the difference between a share-cropper and a labourer remains only in name. Last but not least, the enforcibility of the minimum labour intensity provision of a contract was questioned.[12]

However, after Cheung's work, the number of theoretical contri-butions to sharecropping theory has increased greatly. These works generally follow one of two lines: the inefficiency line or the efficiency line.

The first school follows the traditional argument, in the form of different models, and argues that sharecropping is inefficient. An outstanding example is Bardhan and Srinivasan's work which extends the traditional partial equilibrium analysis to a fairly complete general equilibrium model.[13]

In this model, the tenant himself decides about the labour inten-sity of the sharecropped land and, like the landlord, maximizes his total utility. The demand for and the supply of the leased land are derived from utility maximization by the tenant and the landlord, respectively. For an exogenously given real wage rate, the supply and the demand determine both the rental share and the size of the leased land.

Bell and Zusman (1976) choose another approach which also shows the inefficiency of the sharecropping. First of all, they accept the existence of an excess demand for land in Bardhan and Srinivasan's model which enables the landlords to ration their land.[14] On the other hand, they argue that the difficulty of enforcing

13

a minimum labour intensity limits the power of landlords. Moreover, they argue, tenants and landless labourers are not alike. The former usually own some land, have draft animals, and possess entrepreneurial skills, all of which are hardly obtainable in the local markets of developing countries. Consequently, both the landlord and the sharecropper face market imperfections and are placed in a bargaining situation (Bell and Zusman 1976: 578–81).

Accordingly, Bell and Zusman adopt a bargaining game approach and formulate a model which determines an equilibrium rental share through a bargaining process. Examining the effects of production technologies with zero, unity, and infinite elasticities of substitution between land and labour on the rental share, they show that, given the wage rate, as the elasticity of substitution increases, the landlord has to provide greater incentives for the tenant to work intensively (Bell and Zusman 1976: 585).

In contrast to the above models, the efficiency school tries to prove that sharecropping does not interfere with efficient resource allocation. Boxley (1971) and Newbery (1974) try to show that Cheung's model is correct. Reid (1976) formulates another sharecropping model in which even the tenant, unlike Cheung's tenant, maximizes his income, and like Cheung arrives at a Pareto-optimal equilibrium. In Reid's model, each agent maximizes his total income with respect to those variables over which he has unilateral control, subject to the special constraint that his endowment is fully employed between its alternative uses (Reid 1976: 550–6).[15] The main problem with the model is the assumption that the tenant's labour intensity on sharecropped land is not decided by the tenant himself but by the market and thus the same problem as Cheung's minimum labour assumption may also be raised here.

Hsiao (1975) presents another efficiency model where the equilibrium is reached through a bargaining process with side payments. He argues that if the labour input increases from L_1 to L_2 (Fig. 2.1), the total gain exceeds the total cost for both the landlord and the tenants.[16] This implies that there is a strong incentive for both parts to negotiate. Hsiao concludes that, if monopoly power and negotiation costs are absent, the landlord will compensate the tenant by ABC and the tenant will work up to L_2; i.e. equilibrium moves from A to B which is a stable and efficient equilibrium (Hsiao 1975: 1026–7).

Finally, Lucas (1979) chooses a new approach to the problem. He points out that there is an unrealistic assumption coupled with the sharecropping discussion, i.e. the assumption that a labourer hired to work on a farm will not shirk. In practice, in order to ensure that workers will work hard enough and not shirk, they have to be monitored or supervised. This involves an extra cost and therefore wage contracts are not as efficient as is always assumed. Lucas argues that sharecropping is indeed a way to cope with the labourers' natural tendency to shirk because it gives them an incentive to work diligently and unobserved (Lucas 1979: 504).[17] Consequently, two distortions exist in a system with both share and wage contracts: a tax-equivalent share in the former and a monitoring cost in the latter. Lucas shows that the marginal product of labour in both contracts exceeds the wage rate although they are not necessarily equal (Lucas 1979: 510–11). This means that neither system is efficient and therefore a comparison has to be made between two second-best solutions.[18] This is what Caballero shows in another model that contains a similar argument, concluding, among other things, that labour intensity under share-cropping may or may not be larger than under a wage contract (Caballero 1983: 113).

The disagreement between the two schools is reflected in the empirical studies as well. For example, Johnson provides evidence which shows that there was not much difference between rents per acre of cash-leased and sharecropped farms in Iowa in the period from 1925 to 1946 (Johnson 1950: 118).[19] He believes that such evidence substantiates the efficiency thesis. Heady studies a sample of Iowa farms for the production years of 1949 and 1950 and comes to the opposite conclusion: cropshare farms are cultivated less intensively than the cash-rented farms (Heady 1955). Rao criticizes Heady for not paying attention to the size of the land which was cultivated by each group and thus considers this factor in studying the sharecroppers and owner-operators of West Godavari, India, for 1957–9 (Rao 1971: 590–1). He concludes, in general, that small, owner-cultivated farms were cultivated more intensively than corresponding sharecropped farms while the opposite was true for larger farms (Rao 1971: 591–2).

Cheung gives some evidence from China, 1921–5, which indicates that yields per acre were approximately equal for farms with different tenure arrangements (Cheung 1969: 59). Finally, Bell (1977) suggests that the efficiency hypothesis can be tested more accurately by comparing the difference between input and output per acre on owned and sharecropped plots which are cultivated by the same farmer. Such a comparison for a sample of thirty-one owner-tenants for Purnea, India, reveals that owned plots are cultivated more intensively than the sharecropped land; yield per acre was higher on the former (Bell 1977: 329–35).

Sharecropping, investment and innovation

We have already discussed the adverse effects of the insecurity of tenancy and peasant poverty on the incentive to invest and to innovate (see pp. 9–10). As share tenancy is usually insecure and as sharecroppers are usually poor, one would not expect much improvement in an agricultural sector which is dominated by share-cropping. Beside this, share tenancy has been alleged to inhibit sharecroppers from investing because of the nature of the contract. In fact, a sharecropper who pays 50 per cent of his annual crop to his landlord will find a new method or input attractive if, other things being equal, it can increase the marginal production by more than twice the marginal costs. If output rises less than that, the net return will not even cover the sharecropper's costs and thus he avoids innovation altogether.[20]

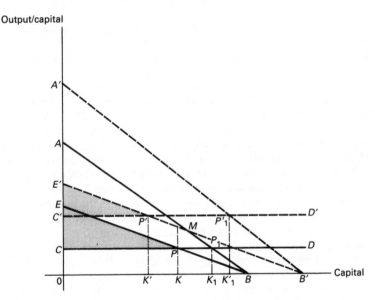

Figure 2.2 Sharecroppers' disincentive for innovation: an illustration
Source: Issawi (1957)

Issawi (1957) illustrates the above argument diagrammatically by using Figure 2.2. In this figure, the horizontal axis represents units of capital and the vertical axis shows output per unit of capital. *AB* depicts the marginal productivity of capital and *EB*, the tenant's share of it. The marginal cost of capital is supposed to be *CD*.

Now, assume that the use of a new kind of equipment raises both the marginal product of capital to $A'B'$ and the marginal cost to $C'D'$, so that $AA' > CC' > EE' = (1-r)AA'$. The tenant's share of the new returns is given by $E'B'$ which would intersect his new marginal cost at P', resulting in input of $0K' < 0K$. The tenant's net income would be $C'E'P'$ which is less than his previous net income, CEP. Since such an investment reduces the tenant's net income, he will be reluctant to invest. On the other hand, the new equipment provides sufficient incentive for an owner-operator, or a fixed-rent tenant to invest. Such an investment increases his net capital return from CAP_1 to $C'A'P_1'$. In other words, although the new investment is profitable under other tenure systems, it is unprofitable for the sharecropper who gives r per cent of the returns to the landlord and pays all the costs. He will be interested in the innovation only if his own share of the increase in unit returns exceeds the increase in unit costs, i.e. $(1-r)AA' > CC'$. In this case, P' will lie to the right of P and the net income of the sharecropper increases.

From Figure 2.2, it can be concluded that sharecropping, by precluding the tenant from innovating, may impose an economic loss on society which is equivalent to the difference between $C'A'P_1'$ and CAP_1. In other words, the net production would have increased by $C'A'P_1' - CAP_1$ if the cultivator had not been a sharecropper and had invested in the new technology (cf. Adams and Rask 1968: 939). This is a loss from the failure to innovate and is different from PMP_1 which results from undersupply of the variable input suggested by the traditional theory. (The area PMP_1 corresponds to the area AJB in Figure 2.1.)

Cheung maintains that if an investment raises the income of the land, it will be made in one of two ways (Cheung 1969: 26). Either the landlord invests in land and charges a higher rental share or he requires the tenants to invest and charges a lower rental share. Since the landowner is the decision maker in Cheung's model, it is he who decides whether or not to innovate in respect to his own interest and irrespective of the impact of innovation on the sharecropper. In fact, in this model innovations and investments leave the tenant's income intact and therefore he may be indifferent to such practices.[21] Moreover, Bardhan and Srinivasan show that when a sharecropper devotes all his labour to sharecropped land, the increase in rental share that follows cost sharing will reduce the tenant's income (Bardhan and Srinivasan 1971: 61–2).[22] Accordingly, such a sharecropper will resist adopting the innovations if they require cost sharing.

If the rental share is given exogenously, tenants will obviously gain from cost sharing and will be encouraged to use variable inputs more intensively. This is what the traditional analysis has recognized for a long time and has suggested that if the landlord shares costs in the same proportion as output is shared, the share-cropper's disincentive to work intensively and invest in land will be eliminated; under certain circumstances, cost sharing may also become attractive to landlords even with exogenously given rental shares (see Adams and Rask 1968: 937–8; Bell 1976). For example, Bell shows that, other things being equal, if an innovation increases the output elasticity of all inputs combined, at the expense of land and draught inputs, and increases production variations, the landlord will be inclined to encourage his sharecroppers to adopt the innovation through cost sharing and therefore its adoption becomes more probable (Bell 1976: 188).[23]

A few remarks have to be made here. We saw earlier that one of the ways which could make sharecropping efficient was to stipulate the minimum labour input, and other non-land inputs, by the landlord and we also discussed the enforceability problems of such provisions (see pp. 12–13). Suppose that the landlord has learned to estimate the tenant's labour input at the harvest. Let us assume further that, other things being equal, technical progress leads to higher output than is available from existing technique while it allows the substitution of land for labour and makes the estimation of labour input very difficult. In such a case, the tenant may be tempted not to apply labour efficiently. Then, the potential extra profit may not be realized and the landlord will resist innovation (see Newbery 1975a: 273). This will especially inhibit innovations that rely on the landlord's support for their adoption. An improvement might also make sharecroppers prosperous and strengthen their power relative to the landlord. Such changes can destroy the political and economic control of the landowner over his tenants and make them more independent. This may also increase his resistance to the new technology even though on exclusively economic grounds the new technology is profitable for him (see Bhaduri 1973: 136). Last but not least, the introduction of innovations which demand cost sharing requires the landlord to play a more active role in farming than is traditionally the case. On the one hand, they have to invest in land, and, on the other hand, they have to supervise their tenants more closely. None of this is likely to be welcomed by traditional landowners.

In the absence of a satisfactory theory of sharecropping, however, it is difficult to decide whether this system is efficient or not, or whether it really inhibits investment in land. For example, if it is efficient, landlords and tenants must be indifferent to alternative tenure systems. Then why do they prefer one to another? And, if sharecropping is not efficient, why has its use become so widespread? This is especially important as one frequently observes the coexistence of different tenure systems in one and the same region.

If we do not believe that people are irrational, the choice of contracts needs explanation. Naturally, they do not prefer one system to another exclusively on economic grounds 'but an economist persists in believing that the "relations of production" ultimately reflect some of the basic economic "forces of production"' (Bardhan and Srinivasan 1971: 48). Attempts to explain the economic reasons for the choice of tenures and the coexistence of different tenure systems reflect such a belief. In the following sections, we examine the theories which try to explain why landlords and tenants prefer sharecropping to other tenure systems.

Sharecropping as risk sharing

A high degree of uncertainty is a distinct feature of production in agriculture. Yields vary greatly from year to year mainly because of uncontrollable variations in the state of nature. Uncertainty is thus an exceptionally important factor for decision making in farming. Such a factor will certainly play a significant role in the choice of tenure, considering the fact that the distribution of risk between contracting parties differs widely between different tenure systems. An owner-operator bears all of the risks of output variations himself while labourers will almost certainly receive their wages. On the contrary, all risks under the fixed-rent tenancy are left to the tenant, the landlord gets his rent and bears no risk. Sharecropping is between these two extremes, risks are shared by both parties; each agent bears a share of risk in proportion to his share of output (see further Griffin 1974: 22–6 and Ho 1976: 88–9).

The risk-sharing capacity of sharecropping has been broadly accepted as an attractive aspect of this tenure system. Using Figure 2.3, Ho shows that the tenant's attitude toward risk affects his choice of contract (Ho 1976). He assumes that each tenant's attitude toward risk is closely dependent upon the position of his income relative to (i) the minimum physiological subsistence level (y_{mp}), (ii) the minimum level required for a standard of living socially and culturally accepted (y_{ms}), and (iii) his desired income (y_D).

The most plausible relationship between these three levels of income is: $y_{mp} \leq y_{ms} \leq y_D$. While y_{mp} can be considered constant, y_{ms}, which is influenced by the average standard of living and other social factors, may change over time. As the economy develops and the standard of living rises, the difference between y_{mp} and y_{ms} increases. It is reasonable to assume that each peasant wishes to reach y_D, but primarily tries to remain above y_{mp} and y_{ms}. The closer he is to y_{ms} or y_{mp}, the greater is the importance of remaining above it. (This is in fact the 'survival algorithm' which was discussed on p. 10.)

Assume further that the tenant knows the mean, μ_Q, and the standard deviation σ_Q, of the output from his past experiences. Consider also that y_f is the tenant's income under a fixed-rent contract with R as rent per unit of land, H. Alternatively, if he sharecrops the land, his income will be y_s. Figure 2.3 shows then how the tenant chooses his tenure system. This figure corresponds to a poor peasant economy where peasants' expected income is normally low and a large variation in output might lead to starvation. y_{mp} and y_{ms} are close to each other and the tenant's average income under both systems is near y_{ms}.

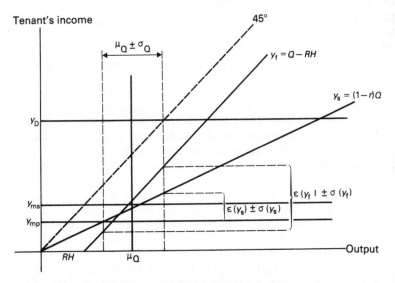

Figure 2.3 Choice of tenure system by a poor peasant

In such a case, a peasant would obviously have a strong aversion to risk and would stick to a system which promises less income variability. As can be seen in Figure 2.3, sharecropping is such a system, and thus the peasant prefers a share contract to a fixed-rent contract even though the latter provides higher expected income.

On the other hand, fixed-rent tenancy would be preferred in a rich economy, or by rich peasants.[24]

Cheung develops a theory of the choice of contract where he combines the risks and transaction costs of different systems (Cheung 1969: 62–72). He argues that any contract involves negotiation and enforcement costs. The contracting parties have to agree about the terms of contract and then check that they are respected. The provisions of a share contract, such as the rental share, the minimum labour input, the farm size, etc., have to be mutually determined and must be controlled thoroughly. In contrast, a fixed-rent tenant or an owner-operator alone decides the amount of the other party's resources he wants to employ at given market prices. This argument implies that the transaction costs of a share contract are higher than those of a fixed-rent or a wage contract. On the other hand, sharecropping offers risk sharing while the other contracts put the risk burden on either party. Cheung concludes that 'the choice of contractural arrangement is made so as to maximize the gain from risk dispersion subject to the constraint of transaction costs' (Cheung 1969: 64). This simply means that a contract is chosen by weighing its transaction costs against its risk, and that, given equal transaction costs, sharecropping is likely to be more widespread in areas of greater uncertainty.

Rao disagrees with the above conclusion (Rao 1971). He believes that greater uncertainty usually reflects a wider scope for entrepreneurship. With a significant scope for decision making, the tenant and the landlord might mutually prefer a fixed-rent contract. This ensures the tenant that he will receive the returns from his entrepreneurial skills and allows the landlord not to become involved in the risks arising from his tenant's decision making. But if the scope for entrepreneurial initiative is limited, the tenant may be anxious to share the uncontrolled risks through a sharecropping contract. The landlord will also accept such a contract provided that the production function does not allow the tenant to restrict the use of non-land inputs (cf. the conclusions of Bell and Zusman (1976: 58) which are explained on pp. 13–14). Accordingly, Rao suggests that a high level of uncertainty brings about fixed-rent tenancy, and sharecropping would be observed more frequently in areas of economic certainty, i.e. where factor substitution and the scope for entrepreneurship are limited (Rao 1971: 593).

Huang (1973) points out that Cheung's theory is not in contradiction with Rao's as long as we distinguish between natural uncertainty and entrepreneurial uncertainty. Natural risks are beyond the control of the tenant. Sharecropping becomes more attractive where these risks are significant. Where the source of risk is peasant decision making and there is potential profit for entrepreneurship, the fixed-rent contract will be more attractive.

The importance of production risks as the principal explanatory factor in the choice of contract is questioned by Stiglitz (1974). He introduces production risks in a general equilibrium model and shows that the risk sharing opportunities that are provided by a sharecropping system are equivalent to the potential benefits from a combination of pure wage and fixed-rent contracts, provided that transaction costs are zero for all contracts (Stiglitz 1974: 236; see also Newbery 1975b, 1977; Reid 1976; Newbery and Stiglitz 1979). Then, other things being equal, production uncertainty is not sufficient to explain the choice of contractual arrangements on its own.

Additional motives for sharecropping

Reid believes that the production flexibility of sharecropping in the face of unexpected events might also provide a partial explanation of the existence of sharecropping (Reid 1976: 570–4). He argues that a crop year has three stages: planting, cultivating, and harvesting. The loss incurred by a setback at one stage can often be reduced by an appropriate response during the remaining stages. An appropriate response can also increase the gain from an unexpectedly favourable turn of events. For example, unexpectedly favourable weather at the beginning of the growing season increases the anticipated yield of a crop. Then, concentrating efforts more on such a crop than on other relatively less-favoured crops may increase the final gain (Reid 1976: 571).

To change the initial plans and undertake the necessary steps usually involves the rearrangement of the contract. Renegotiation costs and potential disagreements over the distribution of the unexpected loss or gain may prevent the contracting parties from proper actions. Unlike a wage or a fixed-rent contract, a share contract has already settled such issues, and both the tenant and the landlord gain from the timely responses. If this is correct, the average productivities of production factors under sharecropping will be higher than under other tenure forms.

Consequently, sharecropping's potential for income enhancement and risk reduction – derived from the encouragement a share contract gives the owners of cooperating factors to similarly respond to surprises – rather than its redundant capability for risk dispersion emerge as a major impetus to share-cropping.

(Reid 1976: 571−2)

Economies of scale and transaction costs are other factors which may make sharecropping preferable to wage and fixed-rent contracts. It should be borne in mind that in the previous section it was concluded that the risk-sharing opportunities provided by a share contract were identical to those that could be provided by a suitable combination of wage and fixed-rent contracts. Now, if there are economies of scale, it appears to be more profitable to have a piece of land under share tenancy than to divide the land into two parcels under two different contracts that together provide equivalent risk dispersion (Newbery and Stiglitz 1979: 330).

Futhermore, the transaction costs of a single contract for share-cropping is probably lower than the total transaction costs of the combination of wage and fixed-rent contracts which would give similar risk sharing opportunities. Accordingly, Reid contends that share contracts would be used because of lower transaction costs, and not in spite of higher contract costs as assumed by Cheung (Reid 1976: 573).[25]

It has also been argued that a sharecropper has a greater incentive than a wage labourer to follow the landlord's instruction whenever he provides managerial expertise (Ho 1976: 92; Reid 1976: 574). It can even be suggested that the farmers who do not want any advice will rent, those wanting some advice will share-crop, and those wanting a lot of advice will work for wages (Reid 1977: 405). Accordingly, tenurial arrangements may operate as screening devices and reflect individuals' abilities (Newbery and Stiglitz 1979: 323−8).

Newbery (1975a, 1977) and Jaynes (1982) try to explain the incidence of sharecropping on the basis of the existence of some factor market imperfection. They, respectively, introduce labour market imperfection and capital market imperfection in their models and find that sharecropping becomes more attractive than other tenurial arrangements.[26]

Finally, Mazumdar (1975) brings up another type of labour market imperfection, namely labour market dualism. Mazumdar's model is based on the assumption that the imputed wage rate for a family member working on a family farm is lower than the current wage rate in many peasant economies.[27] This means that the supply curve of family labour lies below that for wage labour in such economies. Considering this fact, Mazumdar shows that sharecrop-ping is more profitable than self-cultivation for landlords. This can be illustrated with the help of Figure 2.4 which is based on Figure 2.1. *SS* and *S'S'* depict, respectively, the supply curve of labour for the wage labourers and the labour supply curve for family workers.

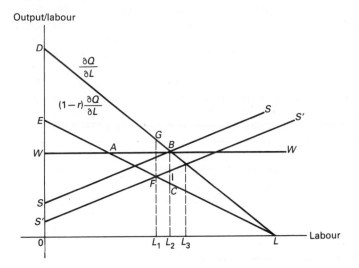

Figure 2.4 The impact of labour market dualism on the choice of tenure system

According to Cheung, the 'net utility' of a worker, i.e. the area *SWB*, is equal to his total satisfaction if he sharecropped the land.[28] But with labour market dualism the supply curve of the share-cropper, who works in the family farm, is *S'S'*. This means that, other things being equal, if the wage worker sharecrops the same farm his net utility increases by the parallelogram *S'SBI*. The land-lord can then stipulate a larger labour intensity, L_3, than he would otherwise do. At the same time he can raise the rental share, *r*, so that the net utility of the sharecropper becomes equal to his alternative net utility, i.e. the area *SWB*. Consequently, sharecropping turns out to be more profitable than own-cultivation by hired labour for Cheungian landlords and all tenure systems are not equivalent as Cheung suggests.

After rejecting Cheung's theory, Mazumdar claims that if labour market dualism is introduced into the traditional theory of share-cropping, it can explain why sharecropping may be preferred to own-cultivation with hired labour in spite of its inefficiency

24

(Mazdumar 1975: 268–71). Let us look at this explanation. We should remember that it is now the sharecropper who determines his labour intensity, as the traditional theory suggests.

When a landlord wants to lease out his land, it is more profitable for him to parcel his land and lease out small holdings. In fact, as the number of tenants rises, the land–labour ratio on the landowner's land decreases and thus the marginal productivity of land in equilibrium increases. The landlord's possibility to reduce farm sizes is, however, limited by the fact that tenants are only ready to sharecrop land if sharecropping provides their alternative net utility, i.e. SWB in Figure 2.4. Suppose that $S'EF$ is equal to SWB and the land is rented free of charge, i.e. $r = 0$. (We suppose for the moment that $EL = \partial Q / \partial L$.) Then tenants are ready to rent any holding which makes the marginal productivity of labour coincide with EL. If the tenant is charged for the land, $r > 0$, the share of the tenant from such holdings falls below EL and the sharecropper leaves the land. Now, the landlord must offer more land to shift the marginal productivity of labour upwards so that the tenant's share of it remains at EL. Consequently, any increase of r has to be accompanied by larger farm sizes. This decreases the total product per unit of land while it increases the landlord's share of it. When these two opposite effects become equal, the landlord's rental income per unit of land is maximized.

Suppose that Figure 2.4 illustrates an equilibrium situation. Then the area $S'EF$, the tenant's satisfaction as a sharecropper, is equal to the area SWB, his net utility as a labourer. On the other hand, the area $EDGF$ indicates the maximum rental income which the landlord can get under sharecropping. He can alternatively cultivate this parcel of land with hired labour and obtain an income equal to WDB. Now, if $EDGF$ is greater than WDB, he will prefer sharecropping; otherwise he cultivates his land with wage labour. The landlord's choice will depend on the values and elasticities of the functions which were referred to in the analysis.

Concluding remarks

Broadly speaking, the traditional agrarian systems are associated with outmoded methods of production, low land and labour productivity, and rural poverty and inequality. This is especially true for the traditional tenancy systems which cover most of the agricultural land and population in developing countries in Asia and the Middle East. The Iranian agrarian system in the early 1960s was, for example, such a system.

Land concentration and absenteeism constitute the core of most of the criticisms of the tenancy systems. Land concentration causes a large proportion of agricultural income to accrue to absentee landlords. Most of this income is transferred to the cities to finance their notoriously luxurious standard of living and their non-agricultural activities. Consequently, nothing or very little is left for investments in the rural areas.

On the other hand, poor tenants do not have much to invest either. Insecurity of leases, which is common in landlord–tenant systems, is likely to preclude further tenants from investing in land. There is hardly any farmer who is ready to invest in land when he is not certain to reap the fruits.

The Iranian landlord–peasant system was criticized for similar reasons. Moreover, since most of the Iranian tenants were share-croppers, it was often presumed that the traditional tenancy systems in Iran suffered from further shortcomings attributed to the share tenancy system. In fact, the conventional theory argued that sharecropping caused land and labour underutilization and deprived peasants of the incentive to apply improvement practices. This view of sharecropping has been challenged recently by a new way of thinking which contends that sharecropping is as efficient as other tenurial arrangements.

Although the ongoing debate concerning sharecropping does not solve the efficiency problem, it reveals some interesting aspects of this tenure system. There is also an interesting tendency to focus on such characteristics of sharecropping instead of the efficiency question. These characteristics will in fact contribute to an explanation of why sharecropping has been observed throughout many parts of the world, including Iran.

It has been argued, for example, that a sharecropping contract might be preferred to the other tenure systems because of the production risks, the conditions prevailing in the factor market, supervision costs, etc. For instance, poor tenants may prefer share-cropping to fixed-rent tenancy when there is uncertainty regarding the avoidance of the damaging consequences of harvest failure. A landlord, on the other hand, might be inclined to opt for share tenancy since this is likely to reduce his supervisory costs, and allow him to increase his income in the presence of labour market dualism, etc. Last but not least, the theory does not offer anything that reduces the main defects of the tenancy system such as insecurity of tenancy and concentration of land in a few hands.

In view of the various criticisms of the traditional agrarian systems such as the Iranian landlord–peasant system, it has been suggested that institutional changes are necessary to pave the way for agricultural growth and improving low levels of living in rural areas of developing countries. Land reform has been proposed as an appropriate means for such changes in, among others, the tenancy system. But before turning to this point, we will examine the pre-reform Iranian agrarian system to see if it really suffered from the problems attached to the traditional tenancy systems.

Chapter three

Pre-reform Iranian village

Having studied the general problems of traditional tenancy systems and discussed the theory of sharecropping in the previous chapter, we now turn to the *arab-raiyati* agrarian system in Iran, which could be considered as a typical tenancy system. We will explore this system to find out whether the Iranian agricultural sector was really faced with sufficient institutional shortcomings to justify an agrarian reform. At the same time, we will recognize the type and extent of the problems that had to be tackled by an agrarian programme that aimed to improve the situation.

On the whole, the pre-reform agrarian system in Iran was characterized by three main features: (i) the concentration of land in the hands of a few absentee landlords; (ii) sharecropping as the major form of land tenure; and (iii) the prevalence of outmoded techniques of production. We will examine these features in some detail, and then focus on rural poverty and inequality, to see how the prevailing agrarian system affected the distribution of income in agriculture and the standard of living of the majority of the rural people in Iran.

Land concentration

On the eve of the land reform programme four different categories of landholdings existed in Iran: private land, state domains, endowed land and crown estates.

Private land

From the Arab Conquest in the seventh century until recently, private land occupied only a small fraction of farm land in Iran.[1] During many centuries the main type of landholding was land assignment. This was called *iqta* or *tuyul*, which was in fact a kind of provisional landownership (Nomani 1980: 201). In this kind of landholding, land or its revenue was granted to government officials, officers and others by the ruler. These grants were given in return for the provision of troops, or instead of a salary, as a pension, or as a gift.[2] In any form, the assignee could hold the land as long as the ruler wished and it could be withdrawn and reassigned at any moment (Lambton 1969: 21). Consequently, the rise and the fall of dynasties, which was not uncommon, economic pressure, etc., caused frequent changes in the composition of the landholding class.

In the nineteenth century, the dominant form of *tuyul* was a land assignment instead of salary, and there was a general tendency for such land to become hereditary. Once the control of the central government weakened a lot of this land was usurped and converted into private property. After the constitution was passed, privatization of lands continued more rapidly. The abolition of the grants of *tuyuls*, which was one of the first laws passed by the first National Assembly in 1907 followed by further legislation in the 1930s, accelerated and legalized this trend. Accordingly, many *tuyul*-holders who controlled large areas became large landowners (Lambton 1969: 129–93).

In the same period, the sale of crown and state land, *khaliseh*, began and continued for many years.[3] These were mainly the result of conquest, inheritance from former dynasties, and confiscation. Thus their volume varied in different periods (Lambton 1969: 27). *Khaliseh* land was under the control of the government which received the rent directly from the peasants (Nomani 1980: 151–61). In the late nineteenth century this type of land was still a major form of landholding. For the most part, however, it was in a state of decay. As *khaliseh* holdings made very little contribution to the finance of the growing public expenditure, it was decided to sell them (Lambton 1953: 152, 239).[4] Until the late 1950s, most lands of this type were sold according to different laws which permitted their sale.[5] However, the peasants were largely unable to buy this land since they were either too expensive or they were taken over by powerful landlords and officials. Besides the landed families, other people such as merchants, contractors, and government servants of all kinds bought most of the lands offered for sale by the government. Thus the sale of state lands ended up with a further concentration of lands in the hands of landlords and the introduction of new elements into the landowning class. These newcomers were mainly after the social prestige of land ownership, while some were also after profit (for more details see Lambton (1953: 240–55); Homan (1955: 286–97)).

As the result of its historical development, the Iranian large landholding class was not a homogeneous one. A large landowner could be a royal family member, a senior army officer, a civil servant, a religious leader or a merchant. He might have only one village or possess tens of villages.[6] In any case, large landowners were altogether a small fraction of the population who controlled quite a large proportion of the villages. These villages were mainly the most prosperous ones, which enjoyed a high annual rainfall or sufficient irrigation facilities (Ashraf and Banuazizi 1980: 18).[7]

Unfortunately, exact statistics about landownership do not exist and the available data are usually guesses, sometimes rather confusing. However, they generally indicate a high degree of concentration of landownership. For example, a sample survey of 1,300 villages near Tehran, the capital, in 1949 reveals that the landlords who had more than 100 hectares represented only 0.2 per cent of the total number of families but owned 34 per cent of the land (see Table 3.1). Considering the fact that landownership in this area was less skewed than other parts of the country, this can be said at best to reflect the nationwide situation (Hadary 1951: 185; Lambton 1953: 281). It is then likely that about one per cent of the rural families owned more than 55 per cent of the land.

Table 3.1 Distribution of land ownership in 1,300 villages surveyed in Tehran and Demavand areas, 1949

Area of land owned (hectares)	% of rural families		% of land
0	60		
0–1	25	} 95	17
1–3	10		
20–100	0.8		22
over 100	0.2		34

Source: Adibi (1955: 149)

There are other estimates which show much higher landownership concentration throughout the country. For example, the Minister of Agriculture was quoted as having said on the eve of land reform that 17,000 villages belonged to the landlords with five or more villages (*Iran Almanac* 1963: 388). It was also estimated that 400 to 500 large landlords owned 57 per cent of all Iranian villages (Keddie 1968: 83).

A large majority of these landlords were absentees. In recent decades there has been a growing tendency among the landowning families to leave the villages and reside in cities and even abroad.

Although some landlords might visit their villages now and then, there were some who never came to their villages.

The property of absentee landlords was supervised by bailiffs and, with growing absenteeism, more and more villages were managed in this way. It was also common for a landlord to lease his land to a third person. The renter could be a non-resident, e.g. a merchant or a contractor, who rented the property for a short period for the profit that he could gain from it. Thus, sometimes even the lessee was an absentee (Lambton 1953: 272).

Not only large landlords but also many medium and small land-owners were absentees. In fact, many of them were new landlords who never lived in the villages. Some others were the heirs of big landlords who were gradually reduced to small landlords because of the subdivision of the land according to Islamic law of inheritance. When such landlords lived in villages, they seldom cultivated their land and they preferred to lease it to peasants (Lambton 1953: 282).[8]

Apart from the different types of landlords, there were some farmers who owned part or all the land they cultivated. However, direct peasant proprietorship was not common in Iran. These farmers usually owned tiny plots which could hardly provide a bare subsistence (Nikayin 1976: 75). On the whole, direct peasant proprietorship might have constituted about 5 per cent of the cultivated land most of which was located in less fertile and isolated areas (Lambton 1953: 277; Kazemi and Abrahamian 1978: 270; Azkia 1986: 89). In some areas, where water was more crucial, peasant proprietors owned their holdings but not the irrigation water. This was often owned separately by a third person who leased it to peasants and enjoyed high income and power (Keddie 1972: 400).

State domains

As we saw earlier, most of the state domains, which were an important type of landholding before the beginning of the twentieth century, had been sold by the early 1960s. As a consequence, the state domains, *khaliseh*, covered only about 3 per cent of all villages before the land reform (*Iran Almanac* 1963: 388).[9] Black observed that most of the public domains were located in very dry, barren lands and in arid mountains (Black 1948: 428). This makes it reasonable to believe that the most fertile lands were sold and became private property, and that mainly the poor land remained in the hands of the government. State domains were not always controlled directly by the government. They were often rented by other persons, e.g. tribal chiefs in Khuzestan, who later let them to the farmers and collected dues as landlords (Research Group 1965b: 161).

Endowed land

Endowed lands, *vaqfs*, were another major type of landholding in Iran. These lands were endowed in perpetuity for some special purposes, either charitable or personal. The benefits of the former were used for the support of religious classes, the maintenance of mosques or shrines, the feeding of the poor, etc. Personal *vaqfs* were virtually private properties because those who endowed lands used the revenues for special personal purposes. According to Islamic law, a *vaqf* cannot be dissolved and it must have an administrator who receives 10 per cent of the benefits for his work. Thus, a person could be the administrator of his endowed land and while using it for his personal purposes, secure it from usurpation.[10] Personal *vaqfs* were also constituted to prevent the subdivision of land because of the Islamic law of inheritance and to escape paying taxes since endowed lands were sometimes exempted from taxation (Nomani 1980: 189).

Vaqf lands were found all over the country, usually mixed with other types of landholdings. They could also appear as the only type of landholding in a given area. For example, it is estimated that about 466 villages belonged to the shrine of Imsam Reza. Most of them were concentrated in Khorasan province (Lambton 1953: 234–5). There is considerable disagreement between the various sources about the amount of *vaqf* lands. For example, one official source estimated that as much as 15 per cent of all cultivated land was *vaqf* while another official source maintains that only 5 per cent of lands were *vaqfs* before the land reform (Dehbod 1963: 62; Momeni 1980: 29).

Vaqf lands were seldom cultivated by their administrators. They were usually leased out to the farmers, or to a third person. Sometimes the administrator rented the land himself. In such a case he paid a fixed amount to the foundation and kept the remainder of the benefit for himself (Lambton 1953: 234).

Crown estates

During the reign of Reza Shah, between 1925 and 1941, an important class of crown lands, known as *amlak*, were the personal property of the ruler. They were separately administered from crown lands proper, which were known as *khaliseh*. These lands were mainly the result of confiscation and usurpation although some of them were apparently 'bought' or were received as 'gifts', or were exchanged for less valuable lands. When Reza Shah was deposed in 1941, he had acquired enormous landed properties and was the largest landowner in Iran. These lands were among the most fertile lands of Iran, e.g. most of Mazandaran province became crown lands during this period (Black 1948: 428; Lambton 1953: 256–7).

After 1941 some of these lands were returned to their former owners. In 1951, Mohammed Reza Shah ordered the redistribution of crown lands among the peasants. The distribution went on for almost ten years and part of the crown lands were sold, partially to the peasants, but mainly to the wealthy landlords and even members of the royal family (Keddie 1972: 399). However, crown villages constituted approximately 2 to 4 per cent of all villages around 1960 (see, for example, *Iran Almanac* 1963: 388; Ashraf and Banuazizi 1980: 17).

To sum up, before the land reform, more than 80 per cent of the cultivated land was concentrated in the form of large private land-ownership, state domains, endowed lands or crown estates. The majority of these lands were let to others for cultivation, mainly under the supervision of a third party. More than 10 per cent of the land also belonged to medium and small landlords who were either absentees or non-cultivating residents. Consequently, a large majority of the rural people were left with no land or not enough land necessary to provide their bare subsistence.

Sharecropping

In spite of the high degree of land concentration, large-scale farming was not common in Iran. Instead, like many other countries in Asia and the Middle East, most of the landowners divided their lands into parcels and leased them to the farmers.[11] The farmers paid a share of the crop, or a fixed rent to the landowner. However, sharecropping was far more common than fixed-rent tenancy. As Table 3.2 shows, about 62 per cent of the total cultivated land was sharecropped while only about 9 per cent of land was leased on a fixed-rent basis.

Although sharecropping was the dominant tenure system in the country as a whole, there were regional variations. For example, we mentioned earlier that peasant proprietors usually dominated in less fertile regions. On the other hand, fixed-rent tenancy was more common in the very fertile region along the Caspian Sea (see Khosrovi 1981: 122, 156; Keddie 1972: 400).

Table 3.2 Numbers and areas of Iranian holdings by type of tenure[a], 1960

Type of tenure	Number of holdings (thousands)	% of all holdings	Area (thousand hectares)	% of total area[b]
Sharecropping	919	49	7,021	62
Owner-operated[c]	692	37	3,353	30
Fixed-rent tenancy	266	14	982	9
Total	1,877	100	11,356	100

Source: FAO, *Report on the 1960 World Census of Agriculture* (1966)

Notes: a The original table contains 204,000 mixed tenures that occupied 1,315,000 hectares. Here, the share of each mixed-tenure category is distributed among the main tenure systems in proportion to their shares of the sub-total.

b Sometimes rounding of percentages causes slight discrepancies here and in the following tables throughout this study.

c It includes both the family holdings which were cultivated by the owners and large estates which were operated by wage labour.

Risk sharing features of sharecropping might have contributed to the prevalence of sharecropping in most parts of Iran.[12] As a matter of fact, Iranian

> agriculture is subject to interruption by the capricious climate. Drought, due to insufficient spring or winter rain, causing partial or total crop failures, and floods after sudden storms, which destroy irrigation channels and *qanats*, are of common occurrence. Earthquakes are another contributory factor, causing local and temporary dislocation. Ravages by pests and locusts not infrequently cause heavy losses. High winds and violent hailstorms are other detrimental factors.
>
> (Lambton 1969: 5)

On the average, one crop in five is likely to be poor or a complete failure; however, two successive bad years or good years are not unusual (Vreeland 1957: 177–8; Land 1965/6: 115).

The dominance of fixed-rent tenancies in the Caspian region may also indicate the importance of production risks in the choice of tenure. It is reasonable to believe that the peasants in these areas, which were generally more prosperous, were more inclined to take risks to achieve higher incomes (see Chapter 2, pp. 19–22, particularly Figure 2.3). However, in the absence of any empirical analysis of sharecropping in Iran, little can be said about the importance of different factors influencing the choice of tenure system in Iranian agriculture.

Cultivation rights and security of tenure

Sharecropping was practised in many different ways all over the country. Customs governed the contracts and there were many regional and local differences.[13] However, they had much in common and their socio-economic consequences were more or less identical.

Generally, only 60 per cent of all rural families received land from landlords for cultivation, mainly on a sharecropping basis. The rest of the rural families were shopkeepers, village artisans, labourers, etc.; these people, who did not have cultivation rights, were called *khwushnishins*. Those who received land and had cultivation rights were called *nasaqdars*. In many places, the cultivation rights of village land were held jointly by *nasaqdars* and usually none of them were entitled to any specific holding in the village. In practice, cultivation rights were hereditary, but they were seldom alienable. Traditionally one of the able sons, usually the eldest, inherited this right. In this way, the subdivision of rights, and thus holdings, which might have resulted following the Islamic law of inheritance was avoided (Khosrovi 1979a: 21).[14] The heirs normally cultivated the land under the same tenurial arrangements as before and there was apparently no relationship between the form of land tenure and individual agricultural skills in Iran. In fact, such a relationship would have appeared if tenurial systems acted as screening devices (see Chapter 2, pp. 22–5).

It is worth noting that the *nasaqdars* did not form a caste. Any villager who knew how to farm and was permanently settled in the village could become a *nasaqdar* with the landlord's consent (Saedloo 1979: 219, 223). This was only possible if the landlord brought new lands under cultivation or if cultivation rights, for some reason, were available for redistribution. Neither of these cases were very common.

Although every sharecropper received a share of the village land, the shares were not necessarily equal. Each sharecropper had a traditionally specified share of the land. The village land was usually measured in terms of plough-lands, or *jufts*.[15] A plough-land was an amount of land which could be cultivated with a yoke of oxen in a farming year.[16] Obviously, the unit of measure varied from place to place and it could be an area of approximately 4 to 6 hectares (Khosrovi 1979a: 16). A sharecropper might have one or several *jufts*, but in many cases he had only part of a *juft*.

The holdings of the sharecroppers were sometimes determined periodically by drawing lots. Consequently, after a year, or some other specified period, the village land was redistributed among the peasants. In each land allotment, each farmer received a holding which consisted of both good and bad lands. Accordingly, village holdings comprised scattered plots that sometimes were very far from each other. Table 3.3 shows the dispersion of average holdings in some provinces.

Table 3.3 Average number of plots in average holdings in five provinces, *c.* 1966

Province	Average size of holding (hectares)	Average number of plots
Gilan	1.8	3
Khuzestan	6.5	6
Mazandaran	4.4	3.4
Sistan and Baluchestan	2.7	4.1
West Azarbayjan	8.7	4.9

Source: Research Group (1965b, 1967, 1968)

Sharecropping contracts were almost verbal and everything depended on the landlord's goodwill, but there were also some traditional checks upon the landlord's arbitrariness. For example, peasants could get a kind of occupancy right if they grew trees, or any other long-lived crop. Periodical land distribution and landlords themselves tended to discourage peasants from planting trees and gaining occupancy rights which could, to some extent, limit the vast power of the landlords. In some places, the peasants owned their houses and their gardens and if the landlord wished to evict them he had to provide compensation; in some areas they had to be compensated for the labour which they put into the land they had cultivated. On the whole, tradition, and in some places the shortage of manpower, limited the extent of peasant eviction in Iran (Lambton 1953: 302; Hadary 1951: 188; Saedloo 1979: 783).

All in all, the allotment system had some egalitarian features. Each peasant had an equal opportunity to get one of the more favourable holdings. Everybody also had access to a share of lands of different qualities. Nevertheless, the system should perhaps be primarily viewed as a means of guaranteeing a bare subsistence and of preventing them from gaining occupancy rights.

Despite all the above facts, the landlords could exercise their power in different ways if they wished to do so. They could transfer a peasant to another area, assign him an inferior holding, and, finally, permanently abrogate his cultivation right to village land (Keddie 1972: 400). Peasants well understood that their means of living were in the hands of the landlords and insecurity was part of their everyday life.[17]

Group farming

The traditional production factors in Iranian villages were land, water, seed, labour and draught animals. In addition to land and water, which a farmer received from his landlord, he was often obliged to hire and rent other factors, too. Some sharecroppers, for example, did not have oxen which were predominantly the main power source and had to rent a team of oxen from an oxen rentier or from a fellow farmer who had one. It was also common for the landlord to provide seed for cultivation. Usually, a sharecropper could not cultivate his holding by himself and had to hire extra hands, especially during the busy periods.

In many parts of the country, for example Qazvin, Kermanshah and Shiraz, sharecroppers did not cultivate their land individually. Instead, they formed a number of groups in each village and each group cultivated the shares of its members from the village land as one big holding. These groups were called *buneh*. Each *buneh* was a co-operative of four to twelve sharecroppers with two to four plough-lands which lasted one farming year. There was a special division of labour among members which mainly reflected their skills and experiences (Safinezhad 1972: 2; Saedloo 1979: 218).

One of the members of each *buneh* was in charge of the activities of the *buneh*. This person, *sarbuneh*, was chosen by the landlord or his bailiff and could keep his position as long as the landlord was satisfied. *Sarbunehs* were normally the most skilled and experienced peasants and kept their position for their lifetime. At the beginning of each agricultural year the *sarbunehs* of a village held a meeting and estimated the amount of land which could be cultivated that year, mainly with respect to the expected water capacity. They decided on the distribution of land among the groups and the water rotation for that year, both of which might be specified by lot. The holding of each group also consisted of scattered plots of varying fertility.

Sarbunehs enjoyed special socio-economic position in the village. They were in the landlords' favour and were more prosperous than the rest of the peasants. Often a *sarbuneh* not only received a larger share of the income of the *buneh* but also had additional incomes such as a yearly bonus from the landlords. As the head of the group, the *sarbuneh* had also some power in the decision making, especially in choosing the members (see further Khosrovi 1979b: 78–92; Hooglund 1982: 24–8; and Safinezhad 1966: 116–17).

Irrigation activities, seed broadcasting, and supervising and directing various activities of *buneh* composed the main part of a *sarbuneh*'s duties. They sometimes chose one or several assistants, according to the size of the *buneh*, to help them with their work. The assistants, *pabunehs*, might have other duties such as weeding the land, as well. At the bottom of each *buneh* were the cultivators, *barzigars*. They were responsible for almost all the hard work of the *bunehs*: ploughing, cleansing water channels, reaping, threshing, etc.[18]

Group farming was in fact a reasonable response to land dispersion and, especially, widespread water shortage in most parts of Iran (Safinezhad 1972: 2; Saedloo 1979: 213–14). The fact that the *buneh* system was more common in dry areas of the country which relied principally on *qanats* for irrigation may reflect the importance of water in the development of group farming. Teamwork would facilitate the construction and maintenance of these underground water channels (Ajami 1975: 141).[19] Moreover, group farming brought about a partial land consolidation and thus made the use of land and water more efficient.

Large landowners could probably run their large landed properties more easily and efficiently through group farming and with the help of *sarbunehs* who had every reason to please their landlords (Ajami 1975: 141; Hooglund 1982: 27). Therefore, they might also have encouraged group farming as a device that was likely to cope with the disincentive problem of sharecropping at a low supervision cost.[20]

Division of the crop

Theoretically, the annual produce would be divided into five equal parts and each part accrued to anyone who provided one of the five traditional production factors: land, water, seed, labour and oxen. In such a case, any sharecropper could capture a share of up to 80 per cent of an unirrigated crop. On the other hand, if the sharecropper could provide only labour and the crop was irrigated, he would receive only 20 per cent of it. In reality, practices differed widely all over the country and the crop was rarely divided into five equal shares.[21] In practice, a sharecropper's portion ranged from extremes of 12.5 to 90 per cent of the crop (Khatibi 1972: 62).

Although the rental shares were apparently determined by custom, it seems that they might have been influenced by the regional values of production factors, the importance of risk which cultivation imposed on each factor owner, the type of crops, and even the bargaining power of each party. Generally speaking, it is likely that the major differences in sharing the crop stemmed from the provision of seed, the irrigation source if the crop was irrigated, and the type of crop (cf. Momeni 1980: 53–7).

The seed supplier, whether the landlord or the peasant, usually received a share that was higher than 20 per cent and, often, up to one third of the crop. (Here, we are mainly concerned with wheat and barley which were the main staple crops.) This might partly reflect the high cost and risk that the seed owner had to accept. The storage of seed was costly and risky. In past centuries, the villagers were under the permanent threat of nomads, who could plunder them at any time, rival villages or rival groups in the same village, tax collectors, or even the army itself. These, naturally, left their imprint on prevailing custom and this influence has persisted until modern times.[22] Moreover, the seed suppliers risked losing all their seed in the case of a crop failure.

The landlord's share as the supplier of land and water varied from place to place, mainly because of the type of farming. In dry farming, the landlord received not more than 20 per cent of the harvest if he did not provide other factors. On the whole, the crop division was more favourable to the peasants in dry farming. For irrigated farming, the landlord's share increased with the cost of providing water. For example, when a *qanat* or well was used for irrigation, a larger share of the crop accrued to the landlord than in the case of the spring- or river-irrigated crops. Moreover, a greater proportion of the harvest was given to landlords when the *qanats* were deeper and longer, and thus more costly.[23]

Irrigation, manuring, weeding, etc. were different for different crops and thus the sharing of the crop was influenced by the type of the crop. For example, the cultivation of rice needs a great deal of water and when the peasant was responsible for all the other expenses the landlord usually captured up to 50 per cent of the crop (Research Group 1965a: 120).[24] On the other hand, for most of the summer crops and vegetables, manuring and weeding were necessary and peasants usually bore these extra costs. This changed the division of such crops in favour of the peasants.[25]

In some areas, the peasants had to pay certain dues to the landlords in addition to the stipulated shares. Furthermore, the peasants had to pay a share of the crop, sometimes from their own share, to the village officials and craftsmen (Lambton 1969: 26).[26]

Where group farming was common, the crop was first divided between the landlord and the group as a unit. A further division between the members of the group occurred after certain dues, which were the responsibility of the group were deducted. The group's share was subdivided between the members, sometimes equally and sometimes unequally. In a skewed distribution, a *sarbuneh* received higher shares than the others, and even his assistants might get more than the cultivators.[27]

Techniques of production and investment in agriculture

At the beginning of the second half of the twentieth century, Iranian farmers largely used the same agricultural methods as their ancestors had been using for many centuries.[28] Animals and manpower were almost always the main power in the agricultural sector; in 1962 there were about 6,000 tractors in the whole country (*Iran Almanac* 1963: 263).[29] Table 3.4 shows that these were not evenly distributed, and there were places where the peasants relied solely on manpower.[30]

Table 3.4 Kind of power used in agriculture in selected provinces (percentages), *c.* 1960

Province	Machinery	Animals	Machinery and animals	Manpower alone
Gilan	0.5	88	2	9.5
East Azarbayjan	3.5	8.5	1	87
Sistan and Baluchestan	2	61	2	35
Mazandaran	14	66	17.5	2.5

Source: Research Group (1968, 1970a)

While animals might be used for ploughing and threshing, all other tasks were performed by hand. The soil was usually ploughed with a wooden plough drawn by an animal. In some places, cultivation was carried out by spade. Digging by spade, which was more common in orchards and vegetable cultivation, required a great deal of manpower. However, it dug the soil much deeper. After ploughing, the ground was broken up by either special animal-drawn ploughs or mallets. The farmers usually sowed seed by broadcasting. Reaping was carried out with a sickle; and the grain was carried to the threshing place by animals or simply by the farmer on his shoulder. Threshing was done by a wooden threshing-machine which was also drawn by draught animals, a job which continued days and nights with men and animals working in shifts. The threshed grain was winnowed in the wind using a special form, and finally the grain was cleaned by sifting it with a sieve.[31]

Cultivation with such simple tools demanded long hours of exhausting, hard work. In order to grow one hectare of wheat and barley a farmer had to work 780 hours, of which 190 hours was with a draught animal, to say nothing of one hectare of cotton which required 2,300 hours of manpower, and 80 hours of animal power (Adibi 1955: 133). The peasants had usually no choice but to employ outside hands, especially at harvesting time.

The discussion of traditional tenancy systems in Chapter 2 showed that these systems were subject to certain factors, such as landlord absenteeism and insecurity of tenancy, which could be detrimental to agricultural progress. It seems likely that the prevalence of outmoded techniques of production and lack of improvement practices in pre-reform Iranian agriculture were in general the outcome of such factors.

The landlords who could invest showed little interest in agricultural investment. As a whole, they are often alleged to have had high propensities to consume. Moreover, when they wanted to invest, they had more profitable alternatives in the cities (Momeni 1980: 27). They usually let their bailiffs run the village affairs or leased their villages to rentiers. The former were notorious for feathering their own nests and the latter tended to squeeze out of the land what they could and then abandon it (Lambton 1953: 271–2).

It is safe to claim that *qanats* were the only investment in traditional Iranian agriculture. However, the available evidence indicates that even this kind of investment was on the decrease as more and more landlords became absentees in recent decades. Since the cost of construction and maintenance of *qanats* was heavy, it was in fact only landowners who afforded such work.[32] As a result,

> not infrequently the *qanats* fell into disrepair when the head of the family died and heirs living in the cities or perhaps Europe, demanding even more income, could not or would not use a sufficient part of the returns to maintain the *qanats* or construct new ones if the old ones could not be repaired.
>
> (Black 1948: 432)

Poverty, periodical reallotment, and lack of security might have precluded peasants from making any investment. Even simple improvement practices such as manuring were rarely carried out. About 83 per cent of the land under cultivation of annual crops received no fertilizer of any kind (Mahdavy 1965: 140). Animal dung was used for fuel rather than for manuring. However, orchards and vegetables which were near towns and villages were manured regularly (Wulff 1966: 269–70).[33] This was mainly due to the easily obtainable human sewerage as well as the fact that such peasants enjoyed more security and were even more prosperous. The peasants did all in their power, with the traditional means at their disposal and based on the experience of many centuries, to cope with agricultural pests and diseases. When they knew no way, or wished to make their methods more effective, they appealed to superstition.[34]

Even though the agricultural methods were primitive, they were excellently suited to the prevailing natural and economic conditions of the village. Despite their general resemblance, there was a large variety of different implements which were made for varying conditions (see Wulff 1966: 260–77 and Lambton 1953: 359–78). Hardary writes, for example, that the type of draught animals in use would not be physically able to draw ploughs of heavier design than the primitive wooden instrument (Hardary 1951: 184). It would have been necessary to improve the breed of animals and feeding practices before it became practicable to introduce more advanced equipment. Furthermore, the shallow, narrow, irregular furrows made by these ploughs prevented wind erosion in the treeless plains which made up a large proportion of the country's arable land. If modern ploughs were introduced without the concurrent addition of tree belts or other methods of soil protection, the result would be decreased rather than increased production. Although the practices which Iranian farmers employed to conserve water were limited in scope and had not progressed much in many centuries, they were in line with modern theories of conservation. Such practices included terracing, the use of irrigation *qanats* to prevent evaporation and conserve water, and the protection of certain trees.[35]

Agricultural production and rural income

Insufficient rainfall, poor soil, lack of investment and improvement practices would naturally result in low production and productivity in Iranian agriculture. The first agricultural census shows that outputs per hectare for wheat and barley, i.e. the major staple crops, were 790 and 770 kg, respectively, in 1960; the yields of wheat and barley in the US were, respectively, 1,433 and 1,509 kg per hectare (FAO 1966; see also Statistical Centre of Iran 1966: 127). There are also reports which give a bleaker picture. For example, a list of yield-to-seed ratios, i.e. the weight of harvested crop to the weight of sown seeds, shows that in nineteen cases average yields for wheat from forty-nine different areas were as low as 5–10 to 1 and only three were up to 50 to 1 on irrigated land in the early 1950s, while comparable figures in the US were 75–150 to 1 (Lambton 1953: 364–5. Platt 1970: 22–3).

The available information also indicates that agricultural production grew very slowly before the land reform. A study which has estimated agricultural production in the period 1935 to 1961 concludes that Iranian agricultural production increased so slowly during that period that per capita production declined (Richards

1975: 6). Similarly, a sample study shows that between 1926 and 1961, crop production increased by about 29 per cent while yields per hectare decreased by 22 per cent (Research Group 1962: 137–54).[36]

On the whole, Iranian agricultural production was rather low especially if we consider the number of people who relied on agriculture for their livelihood. In the early 1960s, more than 65 per cent of the total population lived in villages but only about 30 per cent of the gross national income came from agriculture (see Chapter 1, pp. 4–7). A good deal of this produce was paid to the landlords. A share of the remainder went to those who rendered different services to peasants. Sometimes the peasants had to pay artisans who provided services for cultivation entirely from their own shares. Labourers were also paid mainly by the peasants. They had to pay their loans and the interest after harvesting, as well. Finally, what was left was a small proportion of an already meagre crop. Platt quotes from a minister of agriculture asserting that the peasants retained only 25 per cent of what they produced (Platt 1970: 24).

Three different income groups could be distinguished among the peasants. First, there were prosperous peasants who owned all their production factors except land and enjoyed a relatively comfortable life. This usually meant that they could live at subsistence level without borrowing, and could sometimes even invest in an ox or a luxury. They comprised about 5 per cent of all peasants. Second, there were middle-class peasants who constituted between 30 to 40 per cent of all peasants and earned their living without working for others. However, they sometimes had to borrow to meet their needs. The last group, who were in the majority, consisted of poor peasants. These peasants could hardly survive without additional income. Most of them had to work as casual labourers, mainly in towns, during slack seasons and thus had to compete with agricultural labourers (Momeni 1980: 70–5).

Many peasants kept flocks and wove rugs and carpets to supplement their income. Flocks were kept in almost all villages although their size varied greatly because of climatic differences and the availability of pasture. On the border of the central desert, peasants only kept a small number of animals while in parts of the west they depended equally on flocks and agriculture for their livelihood. The milk products often formed an important part of peasant food, and if there was something left, it could be sold. Goat's hair was used in some areas to weave cloth for tents and to make rope, and sheep's wool was used in carpet weaving. Furthermore, their dung was used as fuel or as manure for cultivation (Lambton 1953: 350). The role of flocks and poultry as savings might also have been important. In the case of some disaster, it was possible to sell them and have some cash in hand for immediate needs.

Another source of supplementary income in some parts of the country was rug and carpet weaving. Rugs and carpets were made mainly by female members of the family. In some areas, the main part of the income of the family came from this activity.[37]

Even part of these non-farming products was transferred to land-lords in the form of different dues. In many areas, the peasants had to pay a certain amount of clarified butter, or cash, per plough land or per share of water; in some other places, they had to pay a pasture fee to the landlord (Lambton 1953: 333, 350–8).[38] A sheep or a lamb, some hens, roosters, eggs, or several kilos of milk products, etc., formed other kinds of dues paid to landlords in different parts of the country for varying pretexts. A gift for per-mission to marry, a present at the New Year, presents on other occasions, etc., are other examples of additional dues.[39] In general, it seems that there was a direct relation between the amount of additional dues and the share of the peasants from the crops: the larger the shares they received, the heavier the dues they had to pay under other names (Lambton 1953: 308). Thus, one may conclude that the peasants were generally left with as much of their whole income as would keep them on the border of subsistence (cf. Momeni 1980: 48).

We have to remember that so far we have discussed the lot of the villagers who had cultivation rights, i.e. *nasaqdars*, and ignored that of agricultural labourers.[40] These people comprised about one-third of the rural population and were normally poorer than peasants. Their life seems to have been very hard. In fact, those labourers who managed to work every day during the busy season were lucky 'in the sense that they had fewer days of hunger with which to contend' (Hooglund 1982: 33).

Peasant poverty, indebtedness and the adverse effects of markets

Reports on the state of villagers and rural studies before the land reform generally agree that most peasants were unable to make ends meet despite all their efforts (for some examples, see Momeni 1980: 60–7). In many cases, all the peasants' crops were exhausted long before the new harvest. However, there were great differences between rural incomes from region to region. For example, a sample survey in a number of villages in different parts of the country found that the annual income of peasant families in the south-east varied between $8 and $80 in 1954. On the other hand, the average family income in the prosperous northern provinces of Gilan, Mazandaran and Azarbayjan was $516 (Keddie 1968: 71–2).[41]

However, most of the villagers suffered from hunger and malnutrition. Indeed, the whole rural life was stricken with poverty. Except in rice-growing areas, the most common diet of rural people was bread. Some did not always have enough bread for the entire year. Locusts and clover were the main food of the poorer peasants in a few areas and the rural people in some regions were reduced to eating herbage in bad years (see Keddie 1968: 75 and Momeni 1980: 61–2). Vegetables, root crops, or some fruit might be eaten with bread; meat was used very little.[42] Houses usually consisted of one or more rooms made of mud-bricks. The rooms had no windows and houses might even lack a latrine. Peasant possessions were generally very limited, hardly enough to satisfy their very primary needs.

Many peasants were forced to borrow for their survival. If they managed to maintain a bare subsistence without borrowing, they might be forced to borrow for other expenses such as tools, seeds, and draught animals. In the absence of institutional credits, the peasants had to appeal to landlords, shopkeepers, and money-lenders for loans.[43] The coming harvest was the security for such loans. In most cases no interest was specified but it was hidden in the terms of the contracts. For example, advances and repayments could be calculated at current prices which involved real rent. This was due to the fact that advances were given in the winter when the prices were very high and were repaid at harvest time when prices were at their lowest. Loans were also raised on the condition that the coming harvest would be sold to the lender at stipulated prices. This practice was known as pre-harvest sale and will be discussed below. Irrespective of the type of loan agreement, the interest rates would be very high. Landlords normally provided advances in easier terms, but they financed only a small portion of all the loans.[44]

Reports from several provinces reveal that in 1960 normally 50 per cent of the peasants were indebted and paid at least a 50 per cent interest rate to non-governmental loan sources (see, for example, Research Group 1965a; 1970b). These sources, which supplied 90 per cent of the credit for agriculture, frequently charged interest rates up to 150 per cent (Platt 1970: 30). Borrowing with such high interest rates aggravated the economic situation of the borrowers and, considering their hand-to-mouth economy, perpetuated indebtedness. Besides, the interest rarely remained in villages which implied a further decrease in the investment capacity of rural areas.

Not only the credit market but also the product market was detrimental to the peasants. Clearly enough, the peasants had no, or very little, surplus to sell and still less income to buy anything. However, product market conditions affected them to a certain extent. Their advances and repayments were assessed at current market prices, they had to sell part of their crops to repay their loans or to purchase other necessities, and frequently planted fruit and vegetables for market. In all such cases, they had to deal with monopsonists, either the landlords themselves or, usually, others such as village shopkeepers and city dealers. For a variety of reasons, the villagers were isolated from the outside world and the village market was the only available one.[45] Lack of adequate roads was a major problem in this respect. Many villagers had no roads at all and where there was a rural road it might be closed for parts of the year. The peasant was either unable to reach the outside markets, or was only able to do so at considerable cost. Hence he was forced to accept any price which was offered by the local buyers. On the other hand, when the peasants wanted to buy something, they had to buy from the only village shop, or from peddlers who enjoyed monopoly power. Of course the effects of this monopoly were on the whole insignificant since the purchases of the peasants were normally limited to a few articles such as tea, sugar and tobacco.

Pre-harvest sale of crops was another practice which indicated peasant poverty and a weak position in the markets. The peasants were often forced to sell their crops before harvest, and sometimes very long before it. This was in fact an indirect way of charging interest for the loans and to circumvent the Islamic prohibition against interest (Khatibi 1972: 62). In such contracts, loans were given provided that the whole crop, or a certain quantity of it, would be delivered to the lender at a stipulated price. The price was determined in different ways. It could be specified on the basis of past experience, or at the low level prevailing at harvest time. Sometimes it might be the current price itself. However, prices were mainly set by lenders who even manipulated harvest-time prices in accordance with their own interest (Lodi 1965: 2).

Pre-harvest sale might also have been a way of coping with production risk.[46] Poverty and lack of security measures made peasants very sensitive to crop failure. If this problem arose, there was little that could be done about it. Risk aversion was probably one main reason for pre-harvest selling of fruits and vegetables for two reasons. First, those farmers who grew wheat in addition to fruits and vegetables had recently harvested their staple crop when they agreed to the pre-harvest sale of the latter, i.e. they were not in any urgent need to borrow. Second, in the case of the pre-harvest sale of grain the peasant was supposed to deliver a certain amount of the crop to the buyer (lender). In the event of a poor harvest, he would have to recover this shortfall. In the case of fruits and vegetables any loss was born by the buyer himself (Lodi 1965: 3). Lodi believes that between 20 to 70 per cent of the total production of crops was sold at prices which were 20 to 40 per cent lower than those obtainable in post-harvest sales (Lodi 1965: 1).

In sum, all such factors not only contributed to the persistence of rural poverty in Iran but also to the exacerbation of the situation. There is evidence which indicates that real peasant income in most areas declined between the late 1920s and the early 1960s (Keddie 1968: 70; see also Lambton 1953: 143–5; Keddie 1972: 365–6).

Concluding remarks

The high degree of land concentration was one of the main features of the Iranian landlord–peasant system. The landowners usually leased out their lands in smallholdings, mainly under sharecropping contracts. The landlords and beneficiaries of non-private land appropriated part of the agricultural income and transferred most of it to the cities since most of them were absentees and lived in urban areas. They did not invest in agriculture, with the exception of the construction and maintenance of irrigation systems in certain parts of the country. Even this kind of investment was on the decrease in recent decades.

Generally speaking, the peasants' share of agricultural income was only sufficient to keep them on the edge of subsistence. They had little to invest. In fact, many of them had to borrow to survive. The lenders, who were usually local moneylenders or shopkeepers, charged high interest rates. They also transferred their profits to the cities.

Poverty, however, was not the only obstacle to peasant investment; insecurity of tenancy and periodical land reallotment deprived the sharecroppers of incentives to invest in land. On the other hand, lack of data does not allow any comparison between investment in land under different tenurial arrangements. It is therefore difficult to say whether sharecropping itself was detrimental to agricultural investment or not.

Poverty and indebtedness seems to have been the lot of the majority of the Iranian villagers. Half of all peasant families, or one-third of the rural population, could hardly survive without additional income, for example, from casual work in the cities during the slack seasons. The life of families of agricultural labourers who comprised another third of the rural people was even worse. They had no access to land and relied on the limited work opportunities in agriculture and casual jobs in the cities. The standard of living of the majority of the remaining one-third was perhaps only slightly better.

We can say that the problems of the Iranian landlord–peasant system were in general similar to those of the tenancy systems that were discussed in the previous chapter. As we saw there, most of such problems are generally assumed to result from the shortcomings of the traditional agrarian systems themselves. Accordingly, many observers argue that changing such systems is a prerequisite for an improvement in rural life and for agricultural progress. It is to this issue, i.e. agrarian change, that we turn in the next chapter.

Chapter four

Theoretical analysis of land reform

The argument that agricultural backwardness and rural poverty are principally a consequence of the institutional characteristics of traditional agrarian systems leads many observers to conclude that changing such systems is a necessary step for both agricultural and rural development. In view of the importance of agriculture in developing countries and its role in economic development, some observers have gone on to argue that agrarian change is in fact a pre-condition for economic development in most Third World countries.

Land reform (agrarian reform) is widely recognized as a promising means of producing desirable agrarian change. It is enthusiastically supported by masses of peasants who believe that land reform will improve their living standards. This belief is shared by many economists who argue that land reform can reduce inequality and poverty in rural areas and induce agricultural growth. The aim of the present chapter is to examine this argument with respect to traditional tenancy systems. We will try to lay down an analytical framework within which we can explain the impact of land reform on agricultural development in general and rural poverty and inequality in particular.

Despite the widespread support for land reform, or perhaps because of it, there is no general agreement about the meaning and content of reform. Thus, we will begin this chapter with a discussion of the definition of land reform. This is followed by a brief examination of the political aspects of the reforms. Finally, we turn to the economic analysis of land reform, which comprises most of the chapter. We attempt to see how land reform might change traditional tenancy systems and will analyse the economic consequences of such a change.

Definition of land reform

Land reform is generally conceived to be a programme that is designed to cope with inequality and poverty in the rural areas. This has primarily been understood to be equivalent to land redistribution. However, it has been argued that there are other programmes which can improve the living conditions of peasants and which accordingly should be included in the definition of land reform. Tenancy reforms, which aim at making the terms of tenancy better for the peasants, are the most prominent examples among the alternative programmes.

There has also been a tendency to widen the concept of land reform mainly on developmental grounds. This has originated from a belief that traditional agrarian systems hinder economic development. Accordingly land reform is assumed to be a means of removing the defects of such systems. For example, almost any programme that leads to a change which improves the manner in which land is held or used is sometimes described as land reform (Barlowe 1953: 174). In a similar vein, the United Nations' various reports on progress in land reform provide a still broader definition that covers even those measures that are usually assumed to be complementary to land reform. That is to say, land reform 'also includes the establishment or strengthening of essential governmental cooperative or commercial agencies or services related to agricultural credit, supply, marketing, extension, and research' (UN 1963: iv).

Accordingly, the term 'land reform' has taken on many different meanings. It may mean a simple rent reduction policy, a radical land redistribution, or a comprehensive rural development plan. This lack of a generally accepted definition of land reform has made almost every author who deals with the subject provide his or her conception of land reform (for some examples see Bergmann 1977; Flores 1970; Lipton 1974; Raup 1968). In general, the equity-oriented definitions emphasize changes in land distribution in favour of the peasants while the development-oriented definitions turn out to be the wider ones.

If rural poverty and inequality are supposed to be the main concern of a land reform programme, these wider definitions may cause confusion. They usually include many different programmes which may not have any meaningful effect on rural life.[1] When land is the main source of income with no or little alternative available, restructuring the distribution of land is likely to be the most effective way to improve the lot of the peasantry in many countries.[2] This is not, of course, a sufficient step. Peasants need credit, extension services, etc., and they have to receive services to raise their level of living. These measures, however, cannot basically change income distribution in agriculture by themselves. Therefore, they must be applied to support land reform, not to replace it (Flores 1970: 897).

In the present study, land reform is defined as the takeover of land or landownership from large landowners, the land being subsequently placed at the disposal of small farmers and landless labourers. This definition is close to the common usage of land reform and the generally accepted sense of the term (see Warriner 1969: xiv–xv; Lipton 1974: 269–74). Moreover, it addresses itself more directly to rural poverty and inequality which is the major objective of our study. Other measures that might theoretically improve the living standards of peasants fall outside our definition. Such measures as tenancy reforms, land reclamation and settlement projects, and progressive land tax have largely shown themselves to be of little help to the rural poor. They might be considered as 'substitute policies' when land reform is not feasible.[3]

Land reform usually comprises two phases: (1) expropriation, and (2) the establishment of a new structure that reduces poverty by spreading the benefits of land more equally than before (see further Warriner 1969: 17–22). The new agrarian system may be one in which peasants own their land and cultivate it personally or cooperatively, or one in which land is nationalized and where large-scale farming such as co-operatives and collective farms generally substitute peasant farms. If land reform aims at developing the former system, it is distributive, and when its object is the latter, it is collective. In this study, we consider only distributive land reform.

Political dimension of land reform

Land is the most important source of income and wealth in traditional agrarian systems. In view of the dominant role of the agricultural sector in the socio-economic life of many developing countries, the importance of land normally extends much further than agriculture; land often means political power and social status in the society as a whole. Therefore, land reform which involves the restructuring of patterns of wealth, income, social status and prestige is predominantly political (Raup 1968: 303). It is also politicians who generally initiate the land reform debate.

The politicians who advocate land reform claim that their major motive is the search for social, political and economic equality in society. Their real motives, however, are likely to be more complex

51

than that and reflect the interests of various classes and groups in the society. As a matter of fact, different politicians strive for different types of changes in a traditional agrarian system and the associated power structure.

Political motives can be classified into three broad groups in regard to their ultimate purposes: liberal, populist and socialist. The liberal motive is represented by the urban elites and even some landowners who desire a modern agrarian system which is freed from the numerous traditions that limit their economic activities. Moreover, the urban elites want to be able to reduce the power of landlords and thereby achieve a more equitable distribution of political power. On the whole, these liberal forces do not seek a radical land reform that would completely erode the power of the landlords and limit the size of land property. They use land reform, above all, as a measure by which pressure can be applied to traditional landlords in order to weaken their resistance to changes in the status quo.

On the other hand, populists and socialists support widespread and fundamental land reforms. They want to eliminate entirely the power of large landlords and redistribute social status and political power. Agricultural labourers, peasants, urban middle classes and workers constitute the major social forces that support such land reform programmes.

In spite of their common interest in the abolition of large landlordism, populists and socialists generally aim at different objectives. The populists, for example, want a transformation from the traditional agrarian system to a peasant system, i.e. a family-farm agrarian system. They believe that such a system would act as a bulwark of political democracy and stability. Moreover, they consider family farms to be more efficient.

Socialist objectives, on the other hand, aim at restructuring society as a whole. They consider agrarian changes both as an important part of overall social change and as a means to gain power and consolidate it in order to carry out other changes. Furthermore, they prefer large-scale farming such as co-operatives and collectives. The main justification for the latter is that large farms are considered to be more efficient than small farms. In addition, socialists sometimes argue that co-operation is morally superior to the individual profit motive.[4]

In addition to internal forces, external factors can influence the process of land reform in a given country. Foreign powers may, for example, exert a marked impact on a land reform programme by strengthening or weakening certain forces. They may also attempt to initiate, speed up, slow down, stop, or even reverse a land reform process. This can be done through direct intervention, providing provisional aid and assistance, or via the propagation of ideologies.[5] The example of agrarian reforms and their results in other countries can also to some extent influence land reform activities, especially in neighbouring countries (Bergmann 1977: 21).

To sum up, the land reform question involves different interest groups in society and provokes different reactions. Landlords as a whole oppose land reform activities which endanger the source of their wealth and income. They do their best to thwart land reform programmes. At the other extreme, there are forces which aim at far-reaching changes through land reform and therefore advocate radical reforms. It is eventually the balance of power between different forces in a society which determines whether or not land reform will be introduced, and if it does, how far it will go in redistributing land, and what changes it will ultimately bring about.

Economics of land reform

As we saw in Chapter 2, the traditional tenancy system has been criticized for adversely affecting agricultural investment and innovation, and for the prevalence of rural poverty and inequality in many developing countries. The concentration of land in the hands of a few absentee landlords seems to be a central element in most of the criticisms of tenancy systems. Therefore, land reform is widely considered to be an effective measure which can promote rural equality and prosperity and foster agricultural progress.

Broadly speaking, the explanation is rather straightforward. First of all, land reform redistributes the main source of income in agriculture and thereby brings about a more equal distribution of income. Moreover, redistribution of income presumably occurs in favour of the peasants who live in rural areas. This in turn means that a larger share of agricultural income remains in rural areas and does not go directly to the cities. Lastly, land reform gives peasants secure titles to land which would in turn stimulate investment. It is not then difficult to see that the interaction of these factors might increase investment and innovation in agriculture and raise the living standard of the peasants.

The traditional approach to sharecropping would certainly suggest that there would be a further improvement in agricultural employment, investment, and output as a result of land reform since it would eliminate the disincentive problem of the system (see Chapter 2, pp. 11–19). On the other hand, the modern line, which contends that sharecropping is efficient, would deny such consequences.[6]

Given the lack of a generally accepted theory of sharecropping, it seems rather difficult to deduce the economic outcome from land reform in such a system. We should, however, consider two important points. First, the efficiency line has devoted much effort to show that sharecropping is as efficient as fixed-rent tenancy and owner-cultivation with hired labour. There have also been some attempts to show that sharecropping has certain advantages over these two systems. But, as we will discuss later in this chapter, these advantages are not always valid when comparing sharecropping with direct peasant proprietorship. One can then conclude that transferring the ownership of the land to sharecroppers is likely to leave the levels of production, investment and employment intact according to the efficiency line.

Second, the sharecropping literature has generally concentrated on the production effects of the system and has overlooked the distributional effects. The fact that sharecropping is often associated with skewed income distribution and poverty is rarely brought up. This is probably presumed to be self-evident: unequal distribution of landownership will result in an unequal distribution of income and has nothing to do with sharecropping. As a consequence, there is no reason to believe that the sharecropping theory opposes a more equal distribution of landownership.

On the whole, the prevailing impression among many observers is that land reform can generally cope with the problems associated with traditional tenancy systems. Concerning sharecropping, one can conclude that the efficiency line views land reform as a purely redistributive measure with no efficiency consequences while the traditional line considers that it is also likely to promote better utilization of production factors.

We maintain that it is the post-reform agrarian system which determines the ultimate outcome of land reform. To express it more precisely, if landowners are not powerful enough to prevent the transformation of the traditional agrarian system, a new agrarian system will emerge out of the reform. This new system may be either 'unimodal' or 'bimodal'.[7] Our major hypothesis is that the economic consequences of land reform are closely bound up with which of these systems prevails after the reform. We begin the discussion with the bimodal system.

The bimodal agrarian system

Land reform laws usually specify the maximum amount of land which a landowner can retain for himself and allow the government to expropriate the lands in excess of that ceiling. Moreover, in many countries certain categories of land are exempted from expro-priations such as land belonging to religious institutions and mechanized farms. These, sometimes deliberate, loopholes in the law provide good opportunities for landlords to retain most of their lands. Since landlords are normally free to choose the land that they want to hold, the retained land usually turns out to be among the best.

At the same time, landlords may increasingly evict their tenants and form modern large- or medium-scale holdings. Exemptions of mechanized farms from expropriation, the prospect of increased profitability from new agricultural technologies, attempts to com-pensate the loss of income from the expropriated land by making the best possible use of the remaining land, the need to create an argument against continued land reform, are among the factors that may contribute to persuade the landowning class to substitute owner-cultivation for the tenancy tenure system (see Alexander 1974; Barraclough 1970; de Janvry 1981; Warriner 1969). Although the landowning families, i.e. former landlords or their younger family members, are mainly the managers of the new, modern farms, some merchants, army officers, local and foreign agribusi-ness companies, etc., may succeed in taking over large and medium holdings. On the whole, while the traditional system changes radically, land concentration undergoes only minor changes and large landowners continue to be a very influential class both politically and economically.

Alongside the farms of the large landowners, there will be another sector comprising small farms which belong to small peasant proprietors. They largely consist of the ex-sharecroppers and the pre-reform small peasants. They will only own a small fraction of the arable land. This means that the reform will create two main groups of farmers: large farmers who own and control large holdings, or some large and some medium holdings, and small farmers who own small plots of land.[8] This is what we call a 'bimodal system'.

The bimodal system, factor-price distortions, and misallocation of agricultural resources[9]   Unequal access to land, which is a basic feature of the bimodal system, implies different land prices for the two groups of farmers. Land is relatively abundant for the large farmers and scarce for the small ones. It is then plausible to argue that land is valued relatively lower than its social opportunity cost for the first group while the second group has to pay higher prices for it. Two reasons can be mentioned in this context. First the large farmers set a monopolistic price for land because they are by far the main source of land supply to the local land market.[10] Moreover, small farmers need land much more than large landlords and this makes their demand less elastic. It is then possible for the large land-owners to practise price discrimination, imposing a higher price on small farmers than (implicitly) on themselves (Lundahl 1984: 525).[11]

In the capital market, landowners are able to obtain loans very easily and at lower rates because their wealth and income minimizes the risk of lending to them. Moreover, the socio-political status of the large landowners tends to direct government credit policy to the satisfaction of their interests (see, for example, Barraclough 1970: 910; de Janvry 1981: 156–7). They have their own savings as well. Small peasants, on the other hand, can hardly obtain credit from institutional resources and usually only have access to the local credit market with notoriously high interest rates. Interest rates are high because the local credit sources such as moneylenders and shopkeepers have monopoly power in the market and because the risk of default is high. Large landowners thus pay a price for capital which is lower than the social opportunity cost while the mass of the peasantry pay a price which is certainly higher than the social opportunity cost of capital.

Finally, control of land and credit associated with limited alternative opportunities for off-farm employment open to labour may enable landlords to exercise control over labour as well. In other words, their monopoly power in the local land market provides them with monopsony power in local labour markets. As monopsonists, they limit their labour demand and push down the number of hired labourers and the wage rate below competitive levels. Nevertheless, the large farmers who rely mostly on hired labour may have to pay higher wages than the implicit wage rate for the small farmers who rely mainly on the family members' labour. In some cases, for example, large landowners are legally required to pay a fixed minimum wage rate. On the other hand, family members may prefer to work on the family farms at (implicitly) lower wage rates rather than moving away for a variety of reasons.[12] We may conclude that the wage is lower than its social opportunity cost for both groups, although it is likely that large farmers pay higher rates than the small ones.

The characteristics of factor markets in a bimodal system can thus be summarized as follows:

$$r_b < r < r_s$$
$$i_b < i < i_s$$
$$w_s \leq w_b < w$$

where r, i and w represent social opportunity costs of land, capital and labour respectively. The subscripts b and s are used to show, respectively, the price of similar factors for large and small farmers.

These factor price distortions cause an inefficient resource allocation in agriculture. Large farmers make extensive use of land and capital, which are comparatively scarce in developing countries, but sparse use of labour, which is relatively abundant. The small farmers, on the other hand, are forced to use too much labour for their available land and capital. In other words, large farmers tend to use techniques of production that are too land- and capital-intensive relative to the social optimum while on the other hand, small farmers use too labour-intensive methods. This is an important conclusion. Let us look at this in some detail.

Biased technical progress under the bimodal system A farmer can produce a crop in many different ways. He will naturally choose a method which minimizes his costs in terms of the prevailing relative factor prices. Other things being equal, all producers of a certain crop use one and the same technique in a competitive world because they face similar prices. On the other hand, the farmers choose different methods when they face different factor prices as in the case of a bimodal system.

Suppose that qq, in Figure 4.1, represents an isoquant for cultivating a crop with different combinations of labour (L) and material inputs (M). (For simplicity we assume that there is continuous substitutability between labour and material inputs.) Further, assume that bb_1 represents the relative factor prices for large farmers whose labour cost is relatively more expensive while ss_1 stands for the relative factor prices of small farmers, who pay relatively more for their material inputs. We can easily see that rich farmers choose technique a which employs relatively more capital and less labour than technique β that is chosen by small peasants.

Given factor price differentials, the two groups of farmers may even show different attitudes toward the new methods of cultivation. In other words, an innovation may only be attractive to one group of farmers. This can be explained with the help of Figure 4.1. We have specified five zones in this figure and an innovation may occur in each of these five zones. The adoption of any innovation depends on where it occurs.

Innovations that fall in zone 1 are 'technologically irrelevant' since they use more inputs per unit of output than existing methods. Those in zone 3, the shaded areas, are 'economically irrelevant' given the current prices. The first group of innovations

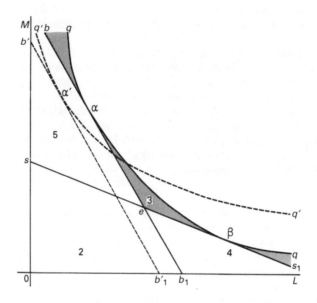

Figure 4.1 Choice of techniques of cultivation

would never be adopted irrespective of the factor prices but the second group are not adopted at present factor prices but may be adopted at certain factor prices. On the other hand, innovations that occur in zone 2, the $0seb_1$ area, will be adopted by everyone.

Any innovation that falls in zone 5, the *seb* area, will be attractive for those who have bb_1 relative factor prices (the landlords), but such an innovation is economically irrelevant for those with ss_1 relative factor prices (the peasants). These innovations could be called 'landord-biased' since only large farmers benefit from them. For similar reasons, new techniques that occur in zone 4, the b_1es_1 area, will only be adopted by small peasants and are therefore 'peasant-biased'. For example, if a new technology is represented by isoquant $q'q'$ it is 'landlord-biased' and will be adopted by large farmers (techniques α') while small farmers will continue to use technique β.

In recent decades, many innovations were only attractive to large farmers since they have been capital-intensive in nature, and thus landlord-biased.[13] This may be explained on two grounds. First, innovations are usually imported from developed countries where labour has not been an abundant factor. Second, research, extension services, and investments in agriculture sponsored by governments, have themselves been landlord-biased. This can partly be explained by the fact that many governments preferred landlord-biased innovations because they have primarily been concerned with raising (explorable) output. Since large farmers control most of the land, 'a landlord-biased innovation could be expected to spread over most of the cultivated surface and have a large impact on production' (Griffin 1974: 51). Moreover, it has been argued in certain quarters that agricultural improvement programmes should be directed towards the large farmers who are more innovative than the small, poor farmers.[14] Finally, where large landowners have remained a powerful class in society they will inevitably influence the government to adopt landlord-biased policies.[15]

The bimodal system, rural poverty, and agricultural growth   The mechanism of the bimodal system will gradually create two quite different sections in the rural economy. At one pole, there would be large farmers who use modern techniques and who produce mainly for the market. The other pole would comprise small farmers who are stuck with traditional methods of cultivation and whose production is mainly subsistence-oriented.

Large farmers are able to follow a 'crash' modernization strategy which is largely based on imported equipment. These imports are usually supported by subsidizing interest rates and undervalued foreign exchange. A key aspect of this modernization process is mechanization, i.e. the use of increasingly agricultural machinery. These are capital-intensive innovations and are welcomed by large farmers to reduce their labour requirement (see Griffin 1974: 67–73). The tendency towards mechanization in large landowners' farms are reinforced by two factors: (1) most agricultural machinery and associated equipment can be readily transferred and their introduction is encouraged by the large international corporations that manufacture them via the provision of suitable service facilities; and (2) the local climate of opinion is often favourable to machinery such as tractors since they are considered to be a symbol of modernity (Johnston and Kilby 1975: 152).

Large farmers produce for the market and can more easily move towards crops that are more profitable. If the profitable crops are cash crops, the small peasants can hardly switch to them because they often do not have access to markets and lack the knowledge and experience of growing cash crops. They cannot afford to buy this know-how either. Moreover, they are likely to be reluctant to run the two additional risks which production of cash crops will impose on them: first the price of the crops may decline or the marketing system may become disrupted and, second, the price of inputs which are necessary for growing the crops may rise or the supply of the inputs may break down (Griffin 1974: 63). Thus, while the prospects of large farmers for increasing their income through cultivating cash crops will probably grow, small farmers will be bound to their subsistence crops.

On the other hand, staple food crops might turn out to be more profitable because it is likely that population growth, growing urbanization, and rising income cause excess demand for food. This would tend to raise the price of food crops and thereby generate increased income for the small farmers whose potentially marketable output is food crops.[16] But there are reasons to believe that price rises may increase income inequality and impoverishment in rural areas. First of all, an increase in the price of food negatively affects landless labourers and deficit farmers who have to buy food considering the fact that real wages will in all probability decline. Second, large farmers who are the main surplus producers will benefit from price rises and the relative stagnation of money wage rates. The marketable surplus of food will then increase by squeezing the consumption of the rural poor and the distribution of rural incomes worsens (Ghose and Griffin 1980: 560–1).

The polarization of the agricultural sector into two sub-sectors is then the most plausible outcome of the bimodal system. Large commercial farms constitute one sub-sector which can enjoy imperfections in the factor market, receive various forms of support from the government, and use new techniques of production. Another sub-sector comprises small peasants and may be adversely affected by all the above factors. Large farmers are able to increase their incomes by both reducing costs and increasing their relatively high price output. Small farmers can hardly increase their incomes and may in fact even experience a fall in their incomes.

Landless labourers and the tenants who are evicted from tenanted land will probably face even greater difficulties. Considering the limited labour demand in rural areas, which might even shrink as large farmers increasingly adopt labour-saving methods, migration will be the only alternative open to these people.

On the whole, there are many factors in the bimodal system which operate against the rural poor. They will even counteract the effects of a secure title to land and a partial redistribution of income which would occur after the redistribution of some land to the peasants. It is not therefore unreasonable to believe that rural poverty and inequality will tend to increase after a land reform that produces a bimodal system. However, the few peasants who can, for one reason or another, advance into the medium-size farmer class or who succeed in getting permanent employment on large commercial farms are likely to experience an increase in their levels of living.

Agricultural production will probably rise, as landlords become actively involved in agriculture and as they, and the newly arrived commercial farmers, invest in land and use modern techniques. However, this rise is not socially efficient and can hardly promote economic development. The rich farmers in fact operate in a system which is subject to factor-price distortions and thus fail to use resources in the most efficient combinations (see pp. 55–7).

Modernization of farming on large farms will also occur in competition with the other sectors of the economy which require foreign exchange to develop. Moreover, if the large farmers specialize in producing cash crops, which are often for export, a large part of the scarce resources in agriculture, land and capital, will be shifted away from the increasingly required food crops. This will reinforce the need to import food crops which puts further pressure on the foreign exchange resources of the country. Finally, the amount of foreign exchange which is spent to cover equipment and food crop imports could even exceed the amount of foreign exchange that large farms earn by exporting cash crops.

The unimodal agrarian system

The post-reform agrarian system would be unimodal if the reform succeeds in transferring all of the land of large landowners to tenants and landless labourers. Landlords might be allowed to retain some land but this would be limited so that the size of their holdings would not exceed that of the average peasants' holdings. A land reform of this kind may lead to an immediate reduction in rural inequality. In other words, agricultural income would be redistributed in favour of the beneficiaries of land reform who are mainly the ex-tenants. They would experience a rise in their standard of living since they retain all of their crops for themselves. They may pay annual instalments for the land they receive but compensation will presumably not be substantial given the favourable conditions for peasants which have been strong enough to promote a radical land reform.

The growing capacity of a system of small-scale family farms might be questioned because of a possible trade-off between equity and capital formation. This is based on the premise that large, rich farmers save a greater proportion of their incomes and therefore can afford to invest in agriculture. In contrast to such an argument some empirical studies show that there is not a meaningful difference between the marginal propensities to save of small and large farmers and, thus, there is no reason to believe that rural saving and investment will be reduced because of such a difference (see Adams 1973: 134).

We even have good grounds for believing that investment tends to increase in a unimodal system. First, land reform stimulates investment and improvement activities since it transfers land ownership to the tenants and secures their rights on their holdings. The farmers are now guaranteed to reap the benefits of their work. This will provide an incentive to increased effort which can lead to higher output and investment.[17]

> The prospect of long and secure tenure may thus create a condition in which maximum incentive is given for investment of family labor time in productive undertakings. Much agricultural capital formation can be explained in this fashion. Livestock care, repair and maintenance of structure, improvement of water supplies, drainage, soil improvement practices, and a variety of similar tasks are often accomplished in agriculture in what might otherwise be leisure time.
>
> (Raup 1968: 274)

Second, even if land redistribution reduces the proportion of income saved, it can increase the volume of savings as the result of increases in the total amount of agricultural output after the reform (Lipton 1974: 291).

The strength of a unimodal system is its capacity to employ the relatively abundant factor, labour, in order to utilize more intensively the relatively more scarce factors, land and capital. In other words, the peasantry generally employs method β in terms of Figure 4.1. It is also 'peasant-biased' innovations which become attractive in this system. The fact that 'output per unit of land is inversely related to farm size' reflects the potential capability of a system of small, family-farms to increase land productivity and output (see, for example, Dorner 1972: 120; Cornia 1985). Redistribution of land among villagers in more equal but still viable holdings can therefore extend the benefits of the reform to some landless families, who do not have access to land, at the same time as it may raise output.[18] 'Viability', of course, limits the number of beneficiaries in densely populated countries. However, a land reform can hardly contribute to the creation of an innovative or happy peasantry if the holdings are too small to provide a decent minimum level of income for the beneficiaries (Lipton 1974: 283).

As peasant incomes rise and their fear of starvation decreases, their capacity to take certain risks and innovate may increase. This can lead to a progressive modernization which implies widespread adoption of a sequence of innovations that is mainly based on simple, cheap implements that can be produced at home. Moreover, there are many agricultural innovations such as hybrid seeds, fertilizer, pesticides, etc. that are technologically scale neutral. Lack of complementary measures like irrigation and credit most often prevent small farmers from applying these inputs in a bimodal system. It is likely that the institutions and government policies which encourage and support the introduction of such inputs, and would probably serve the large land owners in a bimodal system, become peasant-oriented in the unimodal system. Whenever necessary, even indivisible inputs such as irrigation systems and tractors could be made divisible by special arrangements (see Johnston and Kilby 1975: 148–53). All these would facilitate the modernization process in agriculture.

In a unimodal system, all peasants who are confronted with similar climatic and soil conditions are supposed to have approximately equal access to land, water, labour, technical knowledge, etc. If an innovation proves to be profitable to one of these farmers, it is profitable to all the other farmers and it will be adopted rapidly and widely (Griffin 1974: 52). These innovations will be labour-absorbing since their profitability is determined by labour-abundant smallholders.[19] Once the decision to hire tractor services is made by these farmers, there is a good chance that the input will also be a complement to the labour of family members and, in consequence, it will not displace labour (Johnston and Kilby 1975: 149).[20] It is thus reasonable to assume that modernization in this system will increase labour demand which may also improve the lot of some of the landless families.

A small, family-farm system can also further economic development since the total output of the sector is likely to rise. It is important to note that agricultural growth in this system is largely financed by the direct diversion of the small farmers' inactivity, and this hardly affects the nation's resources for financing growth elsewhere (Lipton 1974: 289).

We should observe that the equalization and improvement effects of a unimodal system would be limited under certain conditions. First, although the extent of inequality can be reduced significantly in the rural areas, it does not disappear altogether. Peasants' different initial resources, ability and desire will naturally influence the speed and efficiency with which they can seize new opportunities. Moreover, technological progress will also create differences among peasants since it has an uneven impact on different regions and types of farming. But these differences are not as significant as those in a bimodal system (Johnston and Kilby 1975: 148). In other words, the peasantry will not be polarized between large wealthy, and small destitute farmers.

Second, lack of enough cultivable land normally limits the benefits of land reform to most of the landless labourers who are among the poorest of all villagers. It is true that some of them may benefit from the reform by either receiving land or finding employment as the result of increased labour demand in agriculture. But it is also true that even a highly egalitarian reform which does not intend to create non-viable holdings will only cover a small fraction of landless families in many countries whose agriculture is dominated by a tenancy system (see Lipton 1974: 285–6). Furthermore, subdivision of the larger farms implies reduced levels of employment for landless labourers while the increased labour demand after the reform may fail to provide these people with sufficient employment opportunities. Most of the increased labour demand may be met by increased labour supply of family members.[21] Therefore, alternative employment opportunities in rural areas, e.g. through supporting rural small-scale industries, seems necessary to improve the living standards of these people. The promising opportunity of urban migration would naturally help to alleviate the rural unemployment problem.

The unimodal system and the importance of auxiliary services
Apart from the complementary programme for helping the non-beneficiaries of a land reform, there are also some follow-up services which seem necessary for those who receive land. Over and above land, the new owners need other things: they need credit and advisory services, especially in respect of the utilization of the new inputs. They will also need the help of research and development institutes for the creation of new agricultural inputs and for the testing and adoption of these and imported inputs into the local environment. Moreover, they need marketing and input delivery services, etc. The provision of such services for the peasants will naturally resolve some of their difficulties after the reform and speed up the improvement process which is likely to occur in the unimodal system.

This is not, of course, to suggest that the failure or success of the reform will closely depend on a complicated package of such follow-up programmes. The unimodal system will to some degree guarantee the success of the reform in reducing rural poverty and inequality. First and foremost, this depends on the fact that in our model the unimodal system replaces a traditional tenancy system. In other words, the land reform beneficiary is normally an ex-tenant or an ex-sharecropper who

> already knows about farming; he can now innovate and devote more time to his land, so he needs some extension, but he probably knows how to get it and whether it is worth the effort. Similarly, when his marketing needs change as he moves into surplus, he has some relevant knowledge.
>
> (Lipton 1974: 296)[22]

A problem might arise here with respect to sharecroppers. The study of sharecropping theory in Chapter 2 has shown that sharecropping might offer certain benefits to the contracting parties that other tenurial arrangements might not (see pp. 19–25). It is then likely that sharecroppers lose these 'privileges' when they become peasant proprietors. This may cause some difficulties for them.

As was mentioned earlier, however, most sharecropping models compare this type of tenure system with fixed-rent tenancy and owner-cultivation with hired labour. It is principally within such a context that the advantages of sharecropping appear. However, many of these advantages lose their importance when share-cropping is compared with direct peasant proprietorship. For example, as a peasant proprietor, the land reform beneficiary relies on his own (family) labour which does not as such require super-vision.[23] Moreover, he, himself, is the manager and he would certainly make appropriate responses to unpleasant or pleasant surprises in order to reduce the damage from the former or to increase the gain from the latter. In other words, supervision and production flexibility advantages of sharecropping are of little relevance with regard to peasant proprietorship.[24]

On the other hand, the new owner may face certain problems since he will be deprived of sharing risks through sharecropping and will not have access to, for example, the managerial skills provided by landlords. In view of the increasing absenteeism within traditional tenancy systems, the latter has probably lost most of its significance. It is also reasonable to believe that the risk problem will be less severe after the land reform since the ex-sharecroppers will retain almost all their crops for themselves; as they become more prosperous, they will be less vulnerable to risks. Nevertheless, some insurance against a harvest failure in the years immediately after the reform might be necessary to reduce the extent of the problems that would arise in such a case.

On the whole, one cannot ignore the importance of such programmes. First, the improvement process may be very slow if it is left to itself. The fact that many beneficiaries are indebted and have to repay their pre-reform debts will reduce their investment and innovation capacity over a period of time. Second, lack of alternative ancillary services may give the former rural elite the chance to provide certain services and retain its dominance in another form (Lipton 1974: 296–7). Provision of different services will then accelerate progress in improving the lot of the peasantry and will reduce the risk of the survival of the monopoly powers.

However, the mass peasantry in a unimodal system can probably make their voice better heard and may thus influence the state to provide the necessary services. This will be especially true if the political climate favourable to a radical land reform also persists after the reform.

Concluding remarks

Land reform is usually conceived as an egalitarian measure whose main object is to help the rural poor. The definition at the beginning of this chapter reflects such a belief. The effectiveness of a land reform programme depends, above all, on the political climate of the country. While many different socio-political forces might support land reform, all of them do not advocate radical land reform. Moreover, it is very difficult to overcome the resistance of the landowning class who are usually very powerful in developing countries.

Land concentration in a few hands is the main feature of the traditional agrarian systems in Asia and Latin America. Since land is the major source of income in agriculture, the principal impact of such systems is a highly uneven income distribution in the agricultural sector. A land reform programme is then capable of redistributing income and reducing rural inequality. Moreover, the theoretical analyses indicate that the traditional agrarian systems are likely to be responsible for low output and productivity, rural unemployment and underemployment, and insufficient incentives and/or ability to invest. Consequently, a land reform which changes the traditional agrarian system might also contribute to agricultural development.

Although the micro-analysis concludes that redistribution of land, or landownership, might improve income distribution and promote growth, the actual outcome will largely depend on the kind of agrarian system which develops out of the reform.

A bimodal system emerges when land reform expropriates and

redistributes land on a limited scale but succeeds in compelling and encouraging the large landowners to turn away from their traditional behaviour and become modern agriculturalists. The agrarian system will then be characterized by two different types of farms. On the one hand, there will be small farmers who own small plots of land and, on the other hand, there will be large farmers who own large amounts of land and manage them in the form of large estates or even medium-sized farms. Large farmers enjoy monopoly power in local markets and can influence the government to direct, for instance, agricultural policies towards their interests. They will use modern technology and inputs and can increase their total output and profit. The small farmers, on the other hand, because of their poverty and the prevalence of landlord-biased innovations and government policies, will be unable to change their primitive methods of cultivation. In the final analysis, the new system might contribute to agricultural growth, but it will also increase inequality and poverty in the rural areas. At the same time, production will not be socially efficient since large farmers produce at distorted factor prices.

If the political climate permits a radical land redistribution, the post-reform agrarian system will consist of small family farms. As the peasants own their farms and know that they will retain the results of their effort, they have sufficient incentive to work hard and cultivate their farms as intensively as possible. These farmers have abundant family labour at their disposal and will use it to increase agricultural output and capital. The peasants will then be able to innovate, improve the production methods and inputs. As labour is relatively cheap for these farmers, they will tend to adopt labour-intensive innovations. This will be a general tendency among all peasants since every peasant is faced with more or less similar factor prices and produces in a competitive market. That is to say, a unimodal system might not only benefit the majority of peasants and create growth but it also guarantees the social efficiency of agricultural production. Nevertheless, follow-up services and rural work programmes for surplus labour seem to be necessary for rapid improvements in the levels of living of the rural poor.

Chapter five

An analysis of the Iranian land reform programme

The early appeals for land reform in Iran can be traced back to the early twentieth century. Some minor steps were also taken in this direction by the mid-1950s. For example, as was mentioned in Chapter 3, a royal decree was issued in 1951 for the sale of the crown estates to the peasants. Such attempts had, however, little effect on the Iranian landlord−peasant system and the pressures for agrarian change, especially through a land reform programme, were increasing toward the end of the 1950s.

Consequently, a land reform bill was drafted by the government and an amended version of it was passed by both houses of parliament in 1960. The law was badly drafted and contained many pro-landowner provisions that made it virtually ineffective. A more radical land reform law was then introduced two years later, on 9 January 1962. Although this law was technically an amendation of the land reform law of 1960, it was virtually a new law (Lambton 1969: 63). The land reform law of 1962 was almost immediately put into operation and started the first stage of the Iranian land reform programme. The second and third stages of land reform followed subsequently in 1965 and 1969, respectively, with the implementation of two new amendments to the law.

In this chapter, we want to introduce the basic features of the Iranian land reform programme and examine its contents in order to find out if it could benefit the peasants. As we discussed earlier, this depends largely on the post-reform agrarian system. Therefore, we will try to trace out the land reform laws to see whether they directed the Iranian traditional system toward a pro-peasant, uni-modal or a landlord-biased, bimodal agrarian system.

The present chapter, however, is only concerned with the implications of the land reform laws and other agricultural laws for the development of the new agrarian system. The implementation of the law and the actual consequences of the land reform programme will be discussed in the next chapters. But before analysing the land reform laws, we will look very briefly at the different forces which worked to promote the land reform programme.

A review of the background of the land reform

In the late 1950s, Iran faced a series of social, economic, and political crises. Certain fundamental changes in society seemed unavoidable if the stability of the country was to be maintained. Due to the importance of agriculture in the life of the society, the agrarian question was inevitably a key ingredient of any reform programme.

Between 1955 and 1960, the Iranian economy enjoyed an annual growth rate of about 7 to 8 per cent (Bharier 1971: 45; see also Mahdavy 1965: 135). This growth, which was initiated by increased oil revenues and foreign loans and grants, was accompanied by high public and private expenditures. Imports increased enormously. Most of these imports were consumer goods which might be considered as luxuries or unnecessary at that time. Moreover, they were sometimes in excess of local demands.[1] Investments in trade, construction, and industry increased. Investments were also made in agriculture but these were mainly directed towards large dam projects with doubtful economic returns (Momeni 1980: 163–4; Bharier 1971: 92). But, as inflation began to increase and foreign exchange reserves were depleted, economic problems started to appear. In 1960, the government had to carry out an economic stabilization programme. The volume of internal borrowing, imports and government expenditure was reduced drastically and this resulted in an almost complete stagnation of the country.[2] Meanwhile, signs of discontent were appearing in the urban areas.

As a matter of fact, economic problems in the cities were accompanied by social and political crises in the early 1960s. The increase in urban unemployment, the exacerbation of the living conditions of the urban poor, the widening of the gap between the poor and the rich, and the growth of corruption contributed to create unrest in the urban areas. The established political authority in the country was challenged by both the urban elites, who had gained in strength during the boom years, and the suppressed opposition, which got the chance to operate actively again. Demonstrations and meetings were held in many cities, especially in the capital, although they were treated violently by the government forces (Mahdavy 1965: 134–6; Ashraf and Banuazizi 1980: 25; Momeni 1980: 177–90; see also Zonis 1971: 71–3). On the whole, pressures for changes in the society, not least for changes in the agrarian system, were mounting.

The traditional landlord−peasant system had in fact been criticized from different directions for a long time. It was generally believed that this system was feudal, and that it prevented agricultural development and caused rural poverty. Although the reformation of the agrarian system was demanded by various groups and parties, they often suggested different solutions. For example, some aimed at the abolition of 'feudalism' and redistribution of the landlords' land among the peasants while others believed that the major problem was the landlord−peasant relationship and not the concentration of landownership. Therefore, they argued, it was the latter which had to be changed so that the large landowners became modern agriculturists who cultivated their land with the help of agricultural workers.

There were also certain large landowners who, for a variety of reasons, had been advocating various measures that could change the prevailing situation in the rural areas. Some, for instance, wanted to sell their landed properties if the government could guarantee that they would receive the proceeds from the sale of their land in order to invest it in other sectors. Others wanted to recapture their lands for mechanized self-cultivation, while a third group was anxious about peasant revolution.[3]

The need for change in the conditions of the rural areas was also apparent to the government. Consequently, certain attempts were made to improve conditions for the tenants of the state and crown lands who were now given the opportunity to purchase these lands. However, these attempts to modify the situation progressed very slowly. Moreover, most of the land offered for sale went to people other than the local peasants (see Chapter 3, p. 29 and pp. 32−3).

In contrast to these land sale policies which were supposed to benefit the peasants of certain areas, the government issued two decrees in the early 1950s which concerned all sharecroppers throughout the country. These decrees were in line with tenancy reforms and did not promise meaningful changes in the prevailing system. According to the first decree, 20 per cent of the landowner's share was to be deducted, 10 per cent of which had to be paid to the sharecroppers and the remaining 10 per cent was to be allocated to local development projects. The second decree abolished all the dues that the peasant used to pay to the landlord over and above his share of the crop and limited landlords to using peasant labour or their agricultural implements without payment (for more details, see Lambton 1969: 37−41). However, this government did not last long enough to implement these decrees throughout the country and the subsequent government abandoned both of them.[4]

During the 1950s, landlords generally reduced their investments in irrigation systems because other sectors became much more attractive. For the same reason, traditional moneylenders limited their loans to the peasants. Consequently, both the area under cultivation and production decreased during this period, especially, that of staple crops (see Momeni 1980: 181–2). Living standards in the rural areas deteriorated since the rural share of agricultural production failed to keep pace with the growing population. Although some of the villages that were near big towns and main roads experienced improvement in their economic conditions, poverty remained the lot of the majority (Lambton 1971: 15).

The tendency to blame the landlords for many of the evils in society in earlier years gave place to a campaign of vilification in 1959 and 1960 (Lambton 1969: 55). At the same time, Iran was exposed to strong external pressures for the introduction of a land reform programme. First, the revolution in Iraq in July 1958 had significant repercussions on Iranian political life. On the one hand, Iraq began a land reform programme, and, on the other hand, the revolutionary government put propaganda pressure on Iran (Ashraf and Banuazizi 1980: 26; Momeni 1980: 143). Second, the situation was exacerbated by the numerous radio programmes which launched bitter attacks on the regime.[5] This anti-regime propaganda was especially important because the radio had spread to the most distant villages by 1959 (Lambton 1971: 15). Third, the United States, as the major foreign supporter of the Iranian regime, was urging Iran to carry out a land reform programme.[6] Finally, when most of the countries in the region had had a type of land reform, the absence of any such measures in Iran seemed too conspicuous (Mahdavy 1965: 137).

The government drafted a land reform bill in December 1959 to meet at least part of these pressures. In early 1960, an amended version of the bill was passed by the landlord-dominated parliament.[7] The law, which was already biased towards landlords, contained many loopholes and provisions in their favour.[8] In principle, the law laid down that each landlord could retain only 400 hectares of irrigated land or 800 hectares of unirrigated land. He was permitted to transfer 600 hectares of irrigated and 1,200 hectares of unirrigated land to his heirs. Gardens, woodlands, and land which during the previous two years had been cultivated by mechanized means and agricultural labour were among those categories of land which were exempted from the law. Furthermore, the landlords were able to sell land in excess of the maximum to the peasants, or the government, or retain it and pay an annual tax. In brief, 'the legislators of the Land Distribution Law had thought of every possible way of evading its enforcement and had adopted them' (Land 1965b: 92).[9]

Such an abortive law could hardly bring about any change in a society which was badly in need of change. During August 1960 and May 1961 social unrest led to the fall of two cabinets and the cancellation of the parliamentary election. A new cabinet took office on 6 May 1961, and the newly elected parliament was once again dissolved. The new government declared its intention to struggle against corruption, carry out financial stabilization measures, and introduce a land reform programme.

The new land reform law was declared on 9 January 1962. This law came to be known as 'the law of the first stage of land reform' and was followed by two other laws in the 1960s. These laws, which were in fact amendments to the land reform law, established the framework for the second and the third stage of land reform programme. We will review the main features of the three stages of land reform separately in the following sections.

The first stage of land reform

On 9 January 1962, the land reform law was passed by the cabinet in the form of a decree.[10] There was nothing in the text of the law about the aims of the land reform. However, different government authorities stated that land reform aimed at, among other things, increasing agricultural production, raising the income of the rural people, improving the distribution of agricultural income, and setting free the peasants from the control of the landlords (Research Group 1970a: 51; see also Momeni 1980: 204–5, 217–19; 225–6).

The main features of the land reform law were as follows. (1) Each landlord could retain only one six-*dang* village of his landed property and any land in excess of this maximum was to be sold to government at a given price. (2) The lands which the government bought had to be sold to the peasants who cultivated them on the basis of the existing field layout of the village (*nasaq*). (3) Such peasants could only receive land if they became members of a co-operative society. (4) Fruit orchards, tea plantations, woodlands, 'mechanized lands', and endowed lands (*vaqfs*) were exempted from the law.[11] A Land Reform Organization was set up to carry out the reform under the supervision of a Land Reform Council.[12]

The law declared that all the members of a family that consisted of the wife and dependent children would be calculated as one person. Therefore, they could altogether retain only one whole village. This was confirmed later by the Land Reform Council which decided that the wife and the dependent children could not hold one village each in addition to the head of the family.[13] This decision was reversed during the following eight months and both the wife and each dependent child of a landlord became entitled to hold one whole village each.[14] The new decisions did not affect the lands already distributed to the peasants but they applied to the lands that had been purchased but not distributed (Lambton 1969: 68; Research Group 1970a: 55).

According to the law, a village was the place of residence and work of a number of families who were engaged in farming, where the income of the majority of them came from agriculture, and which was locally recognized as a village. Since the definition was vague and caused difficulties, the Land Reform Council explained more precisely the definition of a village (Lambton 1969: 65–6; Research Group 1970a: 57–8). The Council also tried to limit the choices open to landlords by stating that land reform officials should recommend landowners to sell to the government the villages that had grown into municipalities.[15] However, this decision was modified later and allowed landlords to retain even such villages.[16]

As was mentioned in Chapter 3, there were also large landowners who owned parts of different villages. Considering this fact, the land reform law allowed the landlords to retain six *dangs* of different villages instead of one whole village. Many landlords then planned to redistribute their retained land among several villages in order to maintain their influence in several villages. This was first prohibited by the Land Reform Council but subsequently modified to allow landlords to divide their villages subject to concession made by the regional land reform organizations.[17]

The price of the land which was subject to distribution was to be assessed on the basis of the annual land tax paid by its owner before 1962 multiplied by a special index for each region. This index was determined by the Ministry of Agriculture and was based on, among other things, the distance of the village from cities, the type of crops grown, and the method of division of the crop.[18] The price of the land was paid by the government in ten annual instalments. This was later increased to fifteen.

The government had to sell the purchased lands immediately to the peasants who were cultivating them. These peasants were to pay the government-purchased price plus 10 per cent in fifteen annual instalments.[19] If the land was irrigated, it was to be transferred to the peasants with its traditional water rights.

Finally, the law provided some measures of protection for the peasants of those villages which were either retained by landlords

73

or were not affected by the law. Accordingly, (1) the periodic redistribution of holdings was prohibited (see Chapter 3, pp. 35–6); (2) the peasants were given security of tenure on the land which they were cultivating on the date when the law was passed; and (3) the peasant's share was to be increased by 5 per cent on irrigated land and 10 per cent on unirrigated land and this was to be deducted from the net share of the landowner. The landowner could, however, recover the land for self-cultivation if the peasant agreed to sell his cultivation rights (see further Lambton 1969: 81–4).[20]

It should be mentioned that the law did not define 'mechanized lands'. It only stipulated that the land which was farmed by mechanized means with wage labour on the date when the law was passed would be excluded from the law.

The land reform law of 1962 was immediately put into operation in Maragheh in East Azarbayjan.[21] In fact, lack of trained personnel prevented the Land Reform Organization from carrying out the reform simultaneously throughout the whole country and thus the land reform law had to be executed district by district (Hooglund 1982: 55).[22]

The second stage of land reform

About one year after the implementation of the land reform law of 1962, the government revealed its intention to extend the land reform legislation to the retained villages and the villages owned by small landowners (Lambton 1969: 103–4). The new stage was supposed to mitigate the dissatisfaction of the peasants unaffected by the law and to settle the disputes between the landlords and the peasants.[23]

The new law, which governed the second stage, is known as the Additional Articles. Contrary to the original law, the Additional Articles were put into operation after a long delay. They were first issued on 17 January 1963 but the regulations for their execution were passed by the parliament on 25 July 1964.[24] The implementation of the Additional Articles began on 22 February 1965.

According to the Additional Articles and the regulation for their implementation, the owner of the land which was not affected by the original law had to choose one of five options. He could (1) rent his land to his sharecropper for thirty years; (2) sell the land to the occupying peasants; (3) divide the land between himself and the sharecropper; (4) form an agricultural unit with the peasants; or (5) buy the cultivation rights of the peasants.

Mechanized farms remained exempted from the provision of the Additional Articles. The law defined 'mechanized land' as land which was, at least, ploughed by mechanical means and was cultivated by wage labourers. The charitable *vaqfs* were not exempted at this stage but treated in a special way. They had to be leased to the occupying peasants for ninety-nine years. Personal *vaqfs*, on the other hand, were to be sold to the occupying peasants or rented to them if they did not want to buy the land. Orchards and different kinds of plantations also became the subject of the land reform provided that the occupying peasants had certain traditional rights on them. Such properties were to be sold to the peasants, or bought from them by the landlord, or shared between them in accordance with their respective traditional shares (Lambton 1969: 211–12).

The first method allowed the landlord to lease his land to the occupying peasants for a period of thirty years. The rent was fixed in cash and was based on the average net income of the landowner in the preceding three years. The rent could be revised every five years. If the tenant did not pay the rent within three months of its falling due, the landlord could, with the knowledge of the Land Reform Organization, evict the tenant and lease the land to someone else.

The second option was sale of the land to the occupying peasants. If this method was chosen by the landlord and the peasant, they had to mutually agree on the price and terms of the payment. The government would provide the peasants with a loan of up to one-third of the price of the land at 3 per cent interest. They would start to repay this loan from the sixth year in ten annual instalments.

If the landlord and the peasant agreed on the third method, they had to divide the land between themselves in the same proportion as they traditionally shared the crop. The price of the land was assessed at the highest local coefficient and the peasant had to pay only two-fifths of this price to the landlord.[25] The peasant received a loan to pay one-third of the price and the remainder would be paid in ten annual instalments. The rules for the loans which the peasant received were similar to those under the second option.[26]

The fourth option could only be chosen if the majority of the peasants and landowner(s) in a village agreed on forming an agricultural unit in the village. The unit was to be run by a committee which consisted of three persons: the representative of the landowner(s), the representative of the peasants, and a third person chosen by both the landowner(s) and the peasants. The members of the agricultural unit were to share the proceeds in accordance with local custom (for further information, see Lambton 1969: 204–6).

The last option was in principle one of the provisions of the original law. Accordingly, the landlord could buy the cultivation right of a peasant and farm the land himself if the peasant agreed to the sale. However, the landlord could only buy the peasant out if the land held by the landowner did not exceed a specified maximum limit. This maximum limit was determined by the legislation for different regions and varied between 20 and 150 hectares (Lambton 1969: 206–7).

According to the provisions of the law, landlords could choose the first alternative regardless of peasant wishes. But they could only choose other options if they were able to reach agreement with the peasants. The land reform officials were not supposed to influence the choice of the two parties, but when they agreed on a method, the officials had to be satisfied that the decision was made freely (Lambton 1969: 207–8).

The third stage of land reform

The third stage of land reform began with the implementation of the Law for the Distribution and Sale of Rented Farms in the spring of 1969.[27] It has been argued that this stage was introduced because, (1) the tenants were deeply dissatisfied and there were growing tensions between them and landlords; and (2) some policy makers believed that tenancy inhibited modernization and production growth (see Denman 1973: 143–4; Momeni 1980: 239–40; and Hooglund 1982: 67–9).

This third stage stipulated that the landlords who had rented their lands or formed agricultural units with the peasants were required either to sell their lands to the tenants or to divide the lands between themselves and the tenants. In the latter case, the landowner and the tenant had to divide the land between themselves in the same proportion as they traditionally shared the crop.

When the landlord wanted to sell the land, the price was fixed at ten times the annual rent for cash. The tenant might pay the purchase price in twelve equal annual instalments; in this case the price was twelve times the rent. The cash price of the divided land was equivalent to two-fifths of ten years of rent, minus 15 per cent.[28] The landowners were reimbursed by the government if the peasants defaulted and they could also receive the value of each instalment from the government three months before their due date (Momeni 1980: 240; Hooglund 1982: 69).

Charitable *vaqfs* were exempted from the provisions of this law. Theoretically, *vaqfs* cannot be dissolved, and therefore, they could not be sold to the occupying tenants. But, the civil code permitted the sale of *vaqfs* if the value was enhanced by sale and was then used for the purchase of another property.[29] Accordingly, a law was passed in April 1971 which permitted the sale of these lands to the tenants in accordance with this article of the civil code (Momeni 1980: 241). It was declared that 22 September 1971 was the end of 'one decade of land reform programme'. The lands which were not settled by that date were considered to be sold to the tenants and the rent they paid would be regarded as instalments of the purchase price (King 1977: 409).

Analysis of the land reform legislation, and the government's agrarian attitude and policies

Having reveiwed the Iranian land reforms laws, we now want to examine them in order to see whether they could benefit the rural poor. We have already concluded, in the previous chapter, that a land reform would help the majority of the rural people, and would also contribute to economic development, if it could substitute a unimodal agrarian system for the traditional system. Thus, our main object in this section is to find out whether the laws served the formation of a unimodal system or whether they were 'bimodal-oriented'.

In spite of its shortcomings, the original law of 1962 created favourable conditions for a rapid redistribution of a large part of the land of the large landowners among the peasants. First, specifying one village as the upper limit of landownership and redistri-buting the land among the occupying peasants enabled the rapid implementation of its provisions (Lambton 1969: 64; Warriner 1969: 115). The landlords who would be expropriated and the peasants who would receive the land could be easily specified under the prevailing agrarian system. If the law limited landownership and distributed the land among the peasants in a way which required a cadastral survey and land measurement, it would certainly become a dead letter.[30] Second, we saw earlier that there was a high degree of land concentration in Iran before the reform, and that mechanization was not common (see Chapter 3, pp. 30–1, 40). Accordingly, a large proportion of the agricultural land would have been subject to redistribution. There is a likelihood that more than 30 per cent of the villages were to be redistributed to the peasants during the first stage (cf. Momeni 1980: 248–9). Third, the purchase price might be favourable for the peasants if we consider the fact that in practice landlords paid very low taxes (see Momeni 1980: 230; Hooglund 1982: 53–4).

On the other hand, the first stage was to give land principally to those who cultivated it and the distribution was to occur on the basis of the prevailing village lay-out. In the first place, this would imply that the landless labourers, i.e. about one-third of the rural population, might not receive any land in practice. Furthermore, cultivation rights were not distributed evenly and giving lands to peasants on the basis of these rights would perpetuate the existing inequalities in the villages.

There were also other factors which could limit land redistribution. For example, the land reform, by allowing the landlord to choose which village he would retain, was likely to deprive the peasants of the best lands. This was a serious problem especially when the landlords decided to choose their six-*dangs* from different villages because (i) the landlord was likely to choose the best land in the village; and (ii) he would retain his influence in a large area. Moreover, imprecise definition of a 'six-*dang* village' or lack of a definition of 'mechanized lands' could be used by landlords to evade the law. For example, they could claim that several villages were only one single village and or they could employ a tractor in a village and exclude it from the reform under the pretext of 'mechanized' farming.

As was pointed out earlier, however, the first stage contained pro-peasant elements. Moreover, the anti-landlord political climate which prevailed in the early period of the land reform strengthened the pro-peasant authorities in the government and enabled them to seek ways to limit the landlords' manoeuvres. The landlords were prohibited from dividing their whole villages, the provision of the law which allowed only the head of a landlord family to retain one whole village was confirmed, the definition of the village became more precise, and there were also some attempts to specify and limit the meaning of the 'mechanized lands'.[31]

Although large areas may have remained in the hands of large landowners who owned one or part of one village, we cannot conclude that the agrarian system after the first stage would be bimodal. A bimodal system consists of large and small farmers who compete for scarce resources on unequal terms (see Chapter 4, pp. 54−7). To create such a system in Iran, the landlords had to be able to take over their lands which had been rented out in order to form large and medium-size farms under their own management. The original law generally did not permit such a transformation. According to the law, the retained lands were to remain at the disposal of the occupying cultivators; therefore, they could not become large farms.

A bimodal system was likely to emerge, however, if the landlords could illegally evict the peasants and begin to cultivate their land with hired labour. In fact, lack of peasant participation in the enforcement of the legislation and shortage of trained officials were two factors that could result in slow implementation and evasion of the law. Peasant participation would ensure the effective implementation of the law since peasants knew the local conditions better, they could cope with evasive practices of landlords and reduce the work of the officials.[32]

The necessity of executing the law in one district at a time afforded landowners the opportunity to recover from the initial shock of the reform (Hooglund 1982: 56).[33] The announcement of the draft legislation for the second stage in January 1963 indicated that the opponents of the land reform had finally managed to bring the reform under control. The Additional Articles did not force the landlords to sell their lands but gave them several alternatives and, in practice, they were able to choose whichever alternative they liked best. This seems to have been a pro-landlord move. The subsequent events showed that this was in fact the turning point in the direction of the land reform programme, i.e. a shift from the peasants to the landlords. From then on, two bimodal-biased tendencies emerged in government policies. First, there was a quick move to limit the distribution of land among peasants (cf. Katouzian 1974: 228). Second, landowners, and others, were urged to establish large-scale, modern farms. Both trends are reflected in the changes in some of the regulations of the first stage, the introduction of the second and third stage, and other government agricultural policies.

If we consider the decisions of the Land Reform Council after 1963, we can see that the earlier pro-peasant decisions were replaced by pro-landowner ones. Accordingly, the wife and each of the children of landowners became entitled to one whole village. In other words, a typical family of five could then retain five villages instead of the single village which had previously formed the upper limit. Furthermore, the landlords were permitted to choose parts of different villages as well as villages which had grown and were virtually small towns.

The second stage of the land reform might seem to be in line with a tenancy reform. In reality, the Additional Articles could hardly improve the position of the peasantry. The law in general favoured the landowners at the expense of the peasants. Moreover, there was a long delay between the announcement of the bill, its passing by parliament, and its implementation. The landowners, who had experienced the first stage, were given sufficient time to enable them to take measures to avoid its effects. They could sell or transfer their lands to others, or they could 'mechanize' their lands by ploughing them with a tractor. None of these measures were illegal according to the Additional Articles (Momeni 1980: 236–7).[34] We now turn to the legislation related to the second stage and examine its provisions more closely.

The first method, i.e. tenancy, had certain disadvantages for the peasants. First, the rent, which was the average income of three years, meant that the tenants would pay the same rent as they paid earlier while they were now responsible for all the costs. This was especially important since the landlords' share was normally higher where they provided other services. In such cases, tenants must put up with both higher rents and higher costs. Second, the rent could be revised every five years which would allow the landlord to capture part of a possible production increase of the farms without contributing to the costs or taking any risks. Third, peasants could survive a crop failure under the sharecropping system since they were not required to pay any rent and, moreover, they often received advances from the landlords. In the new system, they both lost this occasional help and had to pay the rent under all circumstances (Momeni 1980: 253). Finally, a bad year might even lead to a peasant's eviction since the law permitted a landowner to abrogate the lease if the tenant fell more than three months behind on payment of the rent (Hooglund 1982: 67). Thus, even security of tenancy, which was apparently the only advantage of the new system, was not seriously guaranteed.

Even selling the land to peasants, the second option, was less favourable to peasants than the first stage. The price of the land and the arrangement to pay the greater part of it were to be determined mutually between landlords and peasants. Given the bargaining power of the two sides, the peasants who received land in the second stage were likely to pay higher prices than those who had received land in the first stage.

The third method, which allowed division of land between landlords and peasants, might benefit the peasants if they had received a large share of the crop. However, the landlord would continue to exert his influence over the village since his share of the whole village could provide him with a large farm. The landlord would, in all probability, also occupy the best lands too. The situation of the peasants in the villages where the sharecropping agreement had been unfavourable to them was likely to be aggravated immediately if this option was chosen. These peasants had to eke out their livelihood on very small, inferior farms. At the same time, they had to pay the instalments for the purchase of the land.

The last two options were also in favour of the landlords. If an agricultural unit was formed in a village, the sharecroppers would farm the land and share the crop with the landlord as before. Thus the agricultural unit was simply a device for preserving the traditional distribution of income from land (Warriner 1969: 124; see also Lambton 1969: 205; Momeni 1980: 253). Permitting landlords to buy peasants out was clearly in contradiction of the main aim of a land reform programme, i.e. land redistribution among the peasants. Interestingly enough, this option also existed in the original law but landlords had not been allowed to use it (see p. 74).

The legislation concerning the third stage of land reform was in fact a shortened version of the previous law. The landlords were to choose either option 2 or option 3 of the five possible methods which were open to them according to the law of the second stage. Considering the later step in selling the *vaqf* lands to the peasants, absentee landlordism must have gone after the reform. Those who owned land were large and small farmers who were to engage actively in cultivation.

The above achievement, by itself, might not be promising from the perspective of the peasants. On the contrary, peasants would be worse off if they had many large farmers beside them. Indeed, this was likely to be the ultimate outcome of the whole Iranian land reform programme. The spirit of the original law was pro-peasant and it initiated a unimodal trend. However, the first stage was not an end in itself. The land reform left the traditional system unaffected in many places.[35] The future of these lands would have a decisive role in the development of the coming system. If such lands were also distributed among peasants, the new system would probably be unimodal. On the other hand, the new system was likely to be unimodal if the landowners could take over all or most of these lands. The subsequent steps of the Iranian reform programme were in line with the latter. Moreover, they even weakened the initial policy by allowing the landowners to retain more lands. The process of moving away from a peasant-oriented system was accelerated further through the changes in the government's attitude toward peasants as well as its agricultural policies. These latter conclusions remain to be explained in detail in the following sections.

The government attitude toward land reform

Broadly speaking, governments usually have two important tasks in a land reform programme. First, they draft land reform legislation and the regulations for their implementation and, second, they are responsible for the implementation of the law.[36] The attitudes of governments towards land reform will thus play a decisive role in the ultimate outcome of the reforms. This is especially true when a government, such as the Iranian one, undertakes full responsibility for formulating and implementing the land reform and denies peasant participation.

As was discussed earlier, the government which took office in 1961 was determined to carry out cetain socio-economic reforms (see p. 72). Land reform was a key ingredient in this programme. Ali Amini, the Prime Minister, considered land reform to be one of its major tasks (Momeni 1980: 204–5). He appointed Hassan Arsanjani as the Minister of Agriculture who was to be in charge of implementation of the land reform. Arsanjani had advocated land reform since 1945 and was known to have radical views on the subject (Lambton 1969: 61–3; Zonis 1971: 54; Hooglund 1982: 42–3, 50–3). Not all the members of the cabinet shared Arsanjani's view and some of them were even against them (Land 1965/6: 97–8, 101). The year 1961, however, provided an opportunity for the advocates of more radical land reform and thus the land reform law of 1962 could be introduced.

When the implementation of the first stage began, the propaganda campaign against the landlords was intensified (Land 1965/6: 101–3; Momeni 1980: 270–5). The government sided with the peasantry and the prevailing impression was that the reform would be extended so that all occupying peasants would receive the land that they were cultivating (see Momeni 1980: 270–5). The principle that land should belong to the tiller was never explicitly stated in the law, but it was announced. Posters with this slogan were put up in the land reform officers in the capital and the provinces (Warriner 1969: 120; Lambton 1969: 100).

The implementation of the law was the responsibility of the Land Reform Organization which was set up under the land reform law. This was a new organization. In a country such as Iran, where many landlords had high government positions and enjoyed great influence in existing institutions, this was an advantage for the reform.[37] Many of the officials in this organization were young and were dedicated to their work. In the early stages they generally enjoyed the confidence of the peasants while they were not welcomed by the landlords (Lambton 1969: 99, 122–3).

Shortly after the beginning of the land reform programme, the cabinet resigned. The new government was less prepared to support the programme in its original form.[38] Arsanjani, however, continued in office. While the land reform was progressing, its opponents could organize and put strong pressure on the government. They mainly used the growing tensions between landlords and tenants in villages not affected by the reform as evidence that land reform was not planned properly (Hooglund 1982: 56). The government showed increasing concern about stabilization in the countryside. The second stage in fact aimed at this goal. Soon after the proclamation of a bill for the second stage, the government was reconstructed and new ministers, who were probably opposed to the land reform, were appointed (see Zonis 1971: 59; Momeni 1980: 284). A high-level economic conference that was subsequently arranged also advocated law and order in the villages as a means for encouraging investment in agriculture (Momeni 1980: 285). The replacement of Arsanjani by an army officer might be considered as a sign that the government was no longer supporting a 'pro-peasant' land reform.[39]

The same change of attitude had also been underway among the land reform officials. The number of these officials had been increasing considerably and there were many officials who were temporarily transferred from other departments of the Ministry of Agriculture (Lambton 1969: 122).[40] The sense of dedication among the officials decreased as their number grew (Lambton 1969: 123). In part, this might have been the result of the extension of landlord influence over this organization in the course of time as well as the arrival of some pro-landlord sympathies from the transferred officials. There were other reasons as well. Security forces, which together with all other military and civilian officials were supposed to help the agricultural ministry to execute the land reform, began to disrupt the work of land reform officials (see Land 1965/6: 107; Zonis 1971: 59). Moreover, the new orders and instructions, which contradicted the previous pro-peasantry ones, disappointed many officials who were working enthusiastically. They were either dismissed or resigned (Momeni 1980: 286).

These changes would naturally slow down and limit land redistribution in those districts where the first stage still remained to be implemented. Moreover, they would further the landlords' benefits from the pro-landlord laws of the subsequent stages.

Agricultural policies and co-operatives

As the government lost interest in land reform as such, it concerned itself more and more with production growth in the agricultural sector. It was believed that modernization, especially mechanization, was necessary to increase agricultural production. This was accompanied by the growing influence of the school which maintained that small peasants lacked capital and experience to increase production. They suggested that the government had to encourage and support men with capital to invest in mechanized farming at the expense of the peasantry (Lambton 1969: 346).[41] In the course of time, this became the core of Iranian agricultural policies. Many agricultural policies such as 'The Agricultural Development Fund', 'Farm Corporations', 'Protection and Utilization of Forests and

Natural Pastures', and 'Establishment of Companies for Development of Lands Downstream of Dams' which were introduced in the subsequent years all urged the creation of large-scale commercial farms (cf. Momeni 1980: 244; Katouzian 1983: 319).

The Agricultural Development Fund was established in 1968 to encourage private investment in barren and dead land. The fund was mainly intended to support the large-scale projects (Denman 1973: 264).[42] The law of 'Protection and Utilization of Forests and Natural Pastures' would in general have similar consequences.[43] This law permitted the government to rent or sell forests and natural pastures in the north of the country to individual persons or companies that wanted to turn them into (large) agricultural enterprises. Some of the machinery they would import was exempted from import taxes (Momeni 1980: 245).

New legislation covering the 'Formation of Farm Corporations' was passed in 1968. Some of the main objectives of the corporations, according to this law, were: (i) to increase the income of the farmers, (ii) to create large-scale mechanized farms, and (iii) to prevent the fragmentation of holdings (see further Freivalds 1972: 185; Richards 1975: 10). Farm corporations were to be established by pooling all the lands of several villages. All farmers in these villages were eligible to be the members of the corporations. This meant that the membership was open to landowners, small peasants, and tenants. A member gave up his land rights permanently and received shares in the corporation mainly in proportion to these rights. He might or might not be employed in the corporations. Employment depended on the need of the corporation.[44]

The government selected the suitable regions for farm corporations and asked the would-be members if they agreed to the setting up of a corporation. The farm would be established when the majority accepted the proposal.[45] Once the formation of corporation was approved, the government would nominate its manager. The government tended to provide generous facilities for the corporation.

A shareholder could sell his shares to other shareholders. Considering the fact that a shareholder was not guaranteed employment in the corporation, small shareholders without employment were likely to sell their shares since the dividend might not meet their ends. Moreover, the general policy of the corporations was to encourage the small shareholders to sell their shares to others or to the corporation (Momeni 1980: 246; Brun and Dumont 1978: 18; Mohammadi 1973: 36). It was then possible that a peasant who had recently received a plot of land of his own sold it back to his former landlord.

The law governing 'Establishment of Companies for Development of Lands Downstream of Dams', passed in 1968, allowed the government to establish very large holdings on lands irrigated by dams. Each holding, known as an 'agribusiness', was to be between 5,000 and 20,000 hectares. Both foreign and domestic investors could receive lands to set up 'agribusinesses'. The government was to provide every incentive to encourage investors, e.g. tax relief, long-term loans, and cost sharing of major construction projects (see Hooglund 1982: 84; Azkia 1986: 225). If there were peasants on the lands involved, the government would buy these peasants out. Considering the huge size of agribusinesses, their development was likely to dispossess thousands of peasants. Thus, the spirit of 'corporations' and 'agribusinesses' was virtually the negation of the original purpose of the land reform programme (Hooglund 1982: 84).

While the government increasingly supported large-scale farming, it provided only limited help for small peasants. This help was supposed to reach the peasants through rural co-operative societies. The stated objectives of these societies were, among others, to provide credit, to buy the agricultural produce of its members; to help the members with storage, transport, and sale of their produce and to provide its members with agricultural inputs and machinery such as fertilizers, pesticides, and tractors (Lambton 1969: 293–4; Momeni 1980: 242–3).

In practice, such multi-purpose societies were few and most of the societies only provided credit for their members. This was of course an important function and would have helped the peasants considerably if it had been worked properly.[46] But the government, which was providing the resources for loans, tended to restrict the total amount of credit to the societies (Hooglund 1982: 109). Moreover, some of the terms of the loans limited further the flow of available credit. For example, new loans were paid to the members of a society only if all the members repaid their previous loans. If one of them defaulted, none of them would receive a new loan (Hooglund 1982: 109–10; Lambton 1969: 314).

The practice of providing only short-term loans to members was also detrimental to the peasants. The members could receive loans for a maximum term of twelve months. This would naturally discourage the peasants from using the loans for productive investment which yielded over a longer period of time. Such investments meant that the peasant had to repay the whole loan from his coming harvest. This was difficult and therefore many peasants preferred to use the co-operative loans for annually recurring agricultural expenses (Hooglund 1982: 110).

On the whole, the general policy of the government tended to limit the scope for co-operative activities. For example, in the first stage of land reform, membership of rural co-operatives was a precondition for receiving land. The policy was to set up separate societies for two to four villages. Each society was to cover between 50 to 300 members (see Hooglund 1982: 106; Lambton 1969: 304). In 1972, the government decided to consolidate the societies so that each society would have more than 1,000 members and would be located in the largest village. This meant that some villages lost their functioning societies (Hooglund 1982: 106). Considering the dispersion of villages and communication problems, many members might in this way have been deprived in practice from the services which they received from their societies.

Concluding remarks

The Iranian land reform programme began in 1962 under both internal and external pressures. This programme passed through three different stages during the 1960s. During the first stage, the reform was pro-peasant although it suffered from certain shortcomings. The reform aimed at limiting large landownership to one village and redistributing the villages in excess of this upper limit among the occupying peasants as quickly as possible. The relatively radical spirit of the law was generally supported by the government. Regulations for the execution of the law and interpretation of its provision were directed towards the peasants and most of the land reform officials did their job enthusiastically. There was considerable hope that a subsequent stage would impose greater restrictions on the landlords and provide more land for the sharecroppers.

However, the landlords were quickly able to regain sufficient strength to control the reform. The introduction of the second stage of land reform, which was the result of a new political situation, reversed the initial peasant-biased policy. In theory, the second stage extended the 'reform' to the retained lands and the lands which were unaffected by the first stage because their owners had one or less than one village. But, in reality, the new law largely secured the property rights of the owners of these lands and encouraged them to abandon the sharecropping system. They were even permitted to buy their tenants out. At the same time, the legislation for the first stage was gradually adjusted so that the upper limit, i.e. one village, was increased. The landowners could now retain more land. These changes, which indicated the pro-landlord attitude of the decision-makers, were accompanied by the weakening of the pro-peasant sympathies among land reform officials. The result of this could increase the benefits of the 'reform' for the landlord beyond the terms of the law.

Meanwhile, the encouragement of the establishment of large-scale modern farms became an important element in the government's general agricultural policy. This was partly due to the belief that only such farms were able to increase agricultural production. On the other hand, small peasants were faced by a growing coolness on the part of the government.

On the whole, many factors seem to have been at work to create a bimodal agrarian system out of the Iranian land reform. Landlords were likely to take over a large, and more fertile, part of their land and cultivate it with the help of agricultural labourers. Some sharecroppers would receive lands of varying, but generally small, size. Some others might be evicted legally, while many more illegally because the prevailing circumstances permitted landlords to engage in such practices. Finally, the third stage of land reform was introduced to force those landlords who still hesitated to give up their old habits either to farm part of their lands themselves or to sell their lands. Legally there was no place for any kind of tenancy.

Chapter six

The agrarian system after the land reform

In Chapter 4, we argued that a distributive land reform may transform a traditional agrarian system into either a 'unimodal' or a 'bimodal' agrarian system. We saw that the economic consequences of these two systems were very different. For example, while the majority of farmers are likely to improve their levels of living in a unimodal system, they would not only fail to do so in a bimodal system but may also experience a fall in their standard of living. This implies that the outcome of a land reform will depend on the kind of agrarian system which develops as a result of the reform. Therefore, we examined the Iranian land reform programme in the previous chapter to see whether it aimed at creating a bimodal or a unimodal agrarian system.

The analysis of the Iranian land reform programme showed that it allowed a rapid redistribution of a relatively large proportion of land in its early stage. This situation, however, lasted only about one year, i.e. until the introduction of the second stage of the land reform programme. From then on, there was a general tendency in the new laws and regulations to limit redistribution and, at the same time, to convince the landlords that they had to give up their traditional form of land use, such as sharecropping. Consequently, it is reasonable to believe that the reform, reinforced by numerous government policies, adopted a bimodal direction. In other words, the post-reform agrarian system in Iran would consist mainly of very small and very large farmers.

In the present chapter, we will seek to present empirical evidence to back up the above conclusions. We will first explore the implementation process of the land reform programme in its three stages especially to find how much land was redistributed among the peasants. As a matter of fact, very few statistics are available with regard to the redistributed land and, therefore, we try to arrive at some reasonable estimates.

On the basis of the above background, we will single out the major characteristics of the post-reform agrarian system in the rest of the chapter. This will pave the way toward an examination of the economic consequences of the reform and its ultimate impact on rural poverty and inequality in the next two chapters.

The implementation of the Iranian land reform

The land reform law of 1962 was put into operation in Maragheh in Eastern Azarbayjan only one week after it was approved by the cabinet.[1] The Government's ambition was to complete the implementation of this law by September 1963. But this plan was not realized and the purchase and distribution of the land which was subject to this law continued even after the introduction and execution of the other stages. These other two stages of land reform were implemented between 1965 and the early 1970s. The whole land reform programme was officially terminated on 22 September 1971. However, the implementation of the reform was not really completed by the date and continued even after 1971.

The amount of land transferred to the peasants during this reform period had obviously a decisive role in forming the new Iranian agrarian system. Since each stage of the land reform had a certain effect on the distribution of land, we will examine the outcome of each stage separately. In this way, we can follow the development of the new system and we will be able to see how powerful large owners managed to save their landed properties and change the direction of the land reform programme.

The first stage of land reform

On the eve of 16 January 1962, when notification was given to the landowners of Maragheh to declare their land, the Minister of Agriculture stated that Maragheh was chosen because its landlords were of the worst type in the country (Land 1965/6: 100). He also said: 'If we can prove that land reform will work in Maragheh, then we have proved that it will work anywhere else' (Land 1965/6: 100). But there might be more plausible explanations. The peasants in this area were economically better off than in many parts of the country. They were good farmers who could immediately benefit from the land reform and exemplify its success. Moreover, the landowners did not have much political power and their position in relation to their peasants had already been weakened. They were likely not to oppose the land reform as hard as those landowners who still enjoyed considerable political power (Lambton 1969: 87–8).[2] On the whole, Maragheh was a 'pilot project' for the

89

government in every respect. The difficulties of enforcing the reform were discovered here. Suitable solutions were then found and passed as legal decrees (Salour 1963: 55–7).

Those authorities who supported the land reform were anxious to begin land redistribution as soon as possible. Thus, when one landowner volunteered to sell her land to the government before the legal deadline, the transfer deed was signed at midnight on 1 March 1962 (Momeni 1980: 271; Land 1965/6: 103).[3] On 12 March, the Minister of Agriculture stated that 99 per cent of the Maragheh landowners had submitted their declarations and the first series of title deeds was handed over to the peasants the next day (Land 1965/6: 103). The implementation of the law was quickly extended to other areas. By the end of 1963 the first stage of land reform had already begun in about twenty-one regions (see Table 6.2, p. 91).

Table 6.1 Progress made in obtaining villages subject to redistribution in the first stage, 1962–75

Period	Number of villages purchased	% of total villages purchased
Jan. 1962–Sept. 1963	8,042	48
Nov. 1963–March 1971	8,109	48
Apr. 1971–Dec. 1975	666	4
Total	16,817	100

Sources: Salour (1963: 58); Bank Markazi Iran, *Annual Report and Balance Sheet* (1965–72); Denman (1978: 266)

The Land Reform Organization made good progress in implementing the land reform up to September 1963. As we saw in the previous chapter, the landlords had succeeded in controlling the reform by this time. Consequently, further implementation of the law was considerably slowed down. For example, in the first half of 1963 the number of villages which were purchased was 4,337 while in the second half of the year only 665 villages were purchased. Table 6.1 shows that the total number of villages which were obtained for redistribution in the first eighteen months of the reform were approximately equal to those which were purchased during the next nine years.[4] This table also reveals that the implementation of the first stage was not completed even in 1971, i.e. when the land reform was officially announced to be finished. It should be noted that there was always an interval between the purchase and redistribution of the eligible villages. Consequently, the first stage was still not completed in 1975; by 1976 some fifty-two purchased villages remained outstanding (Denman 1978: 266).

Table 6.2 Villages purchased in different regions in the first stage up to September 1963

Region	Total villages	Villages purchased	Percentage purchase in the region
1. East Azarbayjan	3,960	1,184	30
1. West Azarbayjan	2,710	285	11
2. Khorasan[a]	6,716	1,133	17
3. Gilan and Shahsavar	2,284	305	14
3. Mazandaran	2,331	261	11
4. Hamadan	665	196	30
4. Kermanshah	2,765	631	23
4. Kordestan	1,681	325	20
4. Salas Shahrestan	599	129	22
4. Zanjan	971	399	41
5. Khuzestan	1,825	459	25
6. Fars	2,779	989	36
7. Arak	479	291	61
7. Central Regions	2,311	337	15
7. Esfahan	1,709	284	17
7. Qazvin	820	159	20
7. Tehran	4,052	240	6
8. Oman Coast	754	16	2
8. Persian Gulf Coast	451	58	13
9. Kerman	5,457	359	7
10. Sistan and Baluchestan	1,283	2	1
10. Yazd	2,000		—
Total	48,592	8,042	16.5

Sources: Research Group (1964); Lambton (1953: 270–1)

Note: a In fact only northern Khorasan belongs to this group while southern Khorasan comes between groups 7 and 8

Some have argued that the first stage was carried out more quickly in regions where landowners were 'larger' since there were fewer landowners to deal with a greater number of villages could be handled in each transaction (Denman 1973: 116–17). Table 6.2 shows that such a statement is incorrect. In this table the names of different regions are listed in the order of their degree of land concentration: number one represents the highest. Those villages which have been given the same number had approximately the same proportion of large landed properties.[5]

We can see that the best results were not achieved in the regions with the highest land concentration, i.e. regions 1, 2, and 3, but in the regions which had a lower land concentration, i.e. Arak (region 7), Zanjan (region 4), and Fars (region 6). In fact, except for East Azarbayjan, only a low percentage of the villages with the 'largest' landowners were acquired. The record of East Azarbayjan was not very high either if we consider the fact that it was here that the law was first implemented and continued to be applied during the most intense phase of the anti-landlord campaign. On the whole, it can be concluded that in the initial and most pro-peasant period of land reform, good progress was only made in the area with a 'medium' degree of land concentration and land fertility.

We should remember that the figures in Table 6.2 refer to the total number of whole and partially purchased villages which were bought in each region. It is estimated that only 37 per cent of these villages, namely about 3,000 villages, were entire, or six-*dang*, villages (Momeni 1980: 309). However, we do not know the proportion of six-*dang* villages in each region. This might limit the above conclusion since a larger proportion of the villages bought in the areas with 'larger' landlords might have been whole villages. We can, however, use Table 6.3 as a good approximation of the whole villages that were purchased in each region. Comparisons of those regions which appear in Tables 6.2 and 6.3 reveal that the proportion of the entire villages was generally not higher in the areas with higher land concentration.

It is interesting to note that between September 1963 and the end of 1975 only about 1,000 whole villages were bought while the number of villages partially purchased increased by about 6,000. In other words, the whole villages acquired for redistribution after September 1963 increased by 33 per cent while the partial villages increased by 120 per cent. This huge increase in the number of villages of less than six-*dang* is not surprising since in March 1963, the landlords were allowed to retain six *dangs* of different villages instead of one entire six-*dang* village (see Chapter 5, p. 73). In all probability, this encouraged many landlords to choose parts of several villages in order to retain the most fertile parts of their landed property as well as to maintain their influence in all these villages.[6]

There is plenty of evidence to indicate that landlords successfully used a variety of subterfuges to retain a large proportion of their land. One method was to transfer the land to relatives or others and to antedate the documents. As early as 20 January 1962 a daily

Table 6.3 Completion of the first stage as of December 1975

| | Villages purchased | | |
Region	6 dang	less than 6 dang	Families who received land
Bandar Abbas	3	13	219
Bushehr	49	132	6,111
Chahar Mahal Bakhtiari	6	102	5,978
East Azarbayjan	510	1,317	123,138
Esfahan	60	338	22,192
Fars	247	1,405	63,307
Gilan	57	690	41,213
Gorgan and Gonbad	2	21	5,990
Hamadan	189	648	80,906
Ilam	210	89	9,547
Kerman	97	454	6,219
Kermanshah	487	1,215	59,013
Khorasan	222	1,069	26,343
Khuzestan	256	452	22,464
Kohkilouyeh and Bouyer Ahmadi	335	43	12,413
Kordestan	166	511	32,145
Lorestan	99	449	16,602
Mazandaran	174	537	69,767
Semnan	10	59	698
Sistan and Baluchestan	1	3	45
Tehran	221	617	50,504
West Azarbayjan	422	435	34,681
Yazd	—	15	82
Zanjan	169	429	20,141
Total	3,992	11,043	709,718

Source: Denman (1978: 268–9)

newspaper, *Kayhan*, wrote that some of the landlords who had over forty to fifty villages had recently transferred part of them to their heirs or sold land to others and consequently reduced their landed properties to less than six villages (cited in Momeni 1980: 288; see also Hooglund 1980: 8). At the beginning of the first stage wives were not entitled to retain any land. Consequently, there were landlords who nominally divorced their wives and transferred part of their land to them (Mohammadi 1973: 32). Another common method used to evade the first stage was to declare falsely that the land had been mechanized and, therefore, exempted from the land reform.[7] In order to justify such a claim, some bought tractors for their farms or, as long as mechanized land was not defined, simply forced the sharecroppers to sign a wage list in order to show that they were labourers (Momeni 1980: 288–9; Platt 1970: 97).[8] After the introduction of the draft of the Additional Articles and its simple definition of mechanized farms, there were landlords who ploughed once with a tractor, which could even be borrowed, and claimed that the cultivation was mechanized.[9] There were also landlords who took the best village away from the peasants and began to cultivate it with tractors.[10]

The exemption of orchards was another loophole which allowed landlords to evade the law. The landlords developed their orchards by appropriating more village land and water. The considerable increase in orchard products between 1960 and 1968 may partly reflect such an abuse of the law. The output of pistachio rose by 600 per cent, apples and pears by 600 per cent, and citrus fruits by 300 per cent (OIPFG 1973: 111; see also Aresvik 1976: 77). There were also landlords who got round the reform by including several villages in one registration unit and retaining them as their 'chosen village'. For instance, a big landlord in Fars declared ten villages as one six-*dang* village and kept all of them (OIPFG 1973: 43–4).[11]

The activities of landlords to retain a large proportion of their land was not limited to the above methods. They tried whatever ways the situation permitted. They bribed the reform officials, forced peasants to leave by bulldozing their houses, deceived peasants to sell their cultivation rights, etc.[12] It seems that many of the landlords' illegal practices were identified but little was done to protect the interests of the peasants, especially after 1963 (see Momeni 1980: 293–5; Lambton 1969: 257–62; Platt 1970: 97; OIPFG 1973: 116–20). Unfortunately, there is no data which can reveal the extent of the land that was retained in this way. However, the estimate given below for the total amount of land redistributed during the first stage suggests that the impact of such actions was far from being limited.

It is almost impossible to determine the amount of land which was distributed among the peasants and all we can find out is the number of the redistributed villages. First of all, Table 6.3 shows that 11,043 out of the total of 15,035 purchased villages, i.e. more than 70 per cent of them, were less than six-*dangs*. A less than six-*dang* village might be anything from a small fraction of the village to almost the whole village. It is therefore not clear how many entire villages were redistributed. Like others, we arbitrarily assume that each partial village is equivalent to half a village on average (see Research Group 1964: 140; Momeni 1980: 266; Katouzian 1974: 229). Accordingly, partially redistributed villages amount to 5,522 entire villages which implies that a total of 9,514 six-*dang* villages were redistributed among the peasants. In other words, about 16 per cent of all Iranian villages were purchased and resold to the peasants under the first stage of the land reform.[13] It is also interesting to note that about 58 per cent of all these villages had been acquired by September 1963 which reflects, more realistically than Table 6.1, the speed of land reform in its earlier period.[14]

According to Table 6.3, a little less than 710,000 families received land in the first stage. This figure is certainly inflated by the practice of many-fold counting. A fieldwork study found out that when only a fraction of a village was sold by one landlord, the entire households of the village were registered as the beneficiaries of the reform and when another landlord sold another fraction of the village, once again, all households were counted to have benefited from the reform (Keddie 1968: 83). In view of this fact, we tried to obtain a more accurate figure by using the average number of families who lived in a village in each region. We ignored the fact that sometimes a large number of the villages were *khwushnishins*, who were practically excluded from land reform, and assumed that in each entire village all families received land.[15] Such a generous estimation shows that about 570,000 families, or 19 per cent of all rural families, might have received some land in the first stage.[16]

The size and quality of the land that the peasant families received varied greatly. This is not surprising since, among other things, the size of the villages differed, their soil quality varied, and the families' traditional shares of the village land were usually not equal. Some maldistribution also emerged as the result of loopholes and illegal practices. It seems that in the early period of land reform, the acquired land was redistributed more equally than the later period. In some cases the enthusiastic officials even gave land to the agricultural labourers (Hooglund 1982: 88–9; Momeni 1980: 316–17; Jones 1967: 114; Lambton 1969: 98).

The second stage of land reform

In contrast to the first stage, the second stage was put into operation long after the introduction of the first draft of its law. When the second stage began after a two-year delay, those landlords who wished to evade the provision of the law had already done so. The implementation of the second stage started in each region when the first stage had been completed and reform officials became available (Lambton 1969: 218).

Although the implementation of the second stage involved considerable office work, most of the work was completed in the first year (see Table 6.4). This, above all, may reflect the pro-landlord

Table 6.4 Implementation of the second stage, February 1965–February 1966

	Villages	*Hamlets*
Land subject to the second stage	52,533	15,166
Land in which the second stage completed	45,513	13,013
Completed cases as % of total	83	86

Source: Lambton (1969: 219)

nature of the second stage. It is likely that the landlords, in general, co-operated with the officials in implementing the law rather than resisting it. In practice, they chose any of the five alternatives which suited them best: they (1) rented their land to the peasants for thirty years; (2) sold the land to the peasants: (3) divided the land between themselves and the peasants; (4) formed agricultural units with the peasants, which implied the persistence of the traditional relationships; or (5) bought out the peasants.[17] The change in the attitude of the government toward the land reform in favour of the landlords certainly contributed to the rapid implementation of the second stage (see Chapter 5, pp. 81–3). The land reform officials now tended to stay in their offices in towns where much of the settlement work was now carried out, sometimes in the absence of the peasants (Lambton 1969: 217; Hooglund 1982: 65). It was also common to ask a team, which was sent to the villages without sufficient preparation, to settle a specific number of villages within one day. They then travelled to the villages which had received no advance notification, rounded up as many peasants as could be found, read the available options and insisted upon immediate decisions (Hooglund 1982: 65).[18]

The statistics concerning the progress of the second stage are puzzling and inconsistent. For example, the statistics for 1966 indicate that 15,024 landlords had bought the traditional right from their peasants. Two years later, the total number of such landlords during all three years was reported to be 7,852! (see Bank Markazi Iran, *Annual Report and Balance Sheet* 1966: 135; Bank Markazi Iran, *Bulletin* 1968). A similar reduction can also be observed in the total number of peasants who had sold their cultivation rights by 1966 and 1972 (see Denman 1973: tables 10 and 10a). The number of landlords and peasants affected by the second stage is another source of confusion in the statistics.[19]

Region	Tenancy (1)[a]		Sale (2)		Division (3)		Corporation (4)		Peasant right sale (5)	
	No.	% of HT[b]	No.	% of HT	No.	% of HT	No.	% of HT	No.	% of HT
Bandar Abbas	299	55	—	—	200	37	—	—	45	8
Bushehr	6,933	74	2,425	26	—	—	—	—	—	—
Chahar Mahal Bakhtiari	22,496	95	128	<1[c]	994	4	—	—	22	<1
East Azarbayjan	179,814	89	13,449	6	7,559	4	1,975	1	46	<1
Esfahan	51,343	68	4,252	6	18,532	25	613	1	464	1
Fars	77,825	44	3,422	2	77,121	44	15,988	9	1,188	1
Gilan	188,536	96	6,313	3	—	—	—	—	—	—
Gorgan and Gonbad	43,135	90	4,761	10	—	—	—	—	564	<1
Hamadan	52,197	72	2,300	3	15,797	22	1,668	2	—	—
Ilam	24,128	100	—	—	—	—	—	—	98	<1
Kerman	3,702	16	22	<1	1,865	8	5,778	25	11,687	51
Kermanshah	48,692	81	392	1	10,679	18	53	<1	185	<1
Khorasan	17,428	23	1,238	2	2,983	4	46,974	62	6,779	9
Khuzestan	79,262	96	24	<1	2,908	4	11	<1	—	—
Kohkilouyeh and Bouyer Ahmadi	32,497	100	—	—	127	<1	—	—	—	—
Kordestan	56,691	93	2,113	3	2,126	3	—	—	97	<1
Lorestan	49,660	87	1,050	2	2,363	4	3,850	7	104	<1
Mazandaran	132,604	99	327	<1	330	<1	—	—	164	<1
Semnan	2,294	94	102	4	—	—	—	—	33	1
Sistan and Baluchestan	254	17	213	14	483	32	22	1	525	35
Tehran	85,203	84	6,101	6	9,136	9	—	—	1,241	1
West Azarbayjan	48,007	79	5,963	10	2,963	5	3,891	6	159	<1
Yazd	18,614	100	—	—	—	—	—	—	—	—
Zanjan	24,948	83	2,569	9	115	<1	2,444	8	—	—
Vertical total	1,246,652	—	57,164	—	156,279	—	83,267	—	23,401	—
% of grand total	80		4		10		5			

Sources: Denman (1973: 338–9); Lambton (1969: 221).

Notes: a Numbers in the parentheses refer to the different options of the second stage.   b Horizontal total.   c The percentage is less than one.

However, we can arrive at a few general conclusions irrespective of the available data that is examined. We have chosen Table 6.5 which shows the number of peasants affected as late as 1972. The last column of the table is corrected with the help of a similar table for 1966. We compared the total number of peasants who sold their cultivation rights and inserted the higher figure in Table 6.5. The rationale is simple: the number of such peasants could only increase or remain constant after 1966.

Table 6.5 shows that alternative (1), i.e. renting the land to the peasant, was predominantly preferred by the landlords in all regions except in Kerman (16 per cent), Sistan and Baluchistan (17 per cent), Khorasan (23 per cent) and Fars (44 per cent). For the country as a whole, about 80 per cent of the cases were settled by the tenancy arrangement. Although the landlords could maintain the traditional sharecropping system in the form of owner–peasant joint stock corporations, only a few chose to do so, except in Khorasan. These facts suggest that the tenancy option was highly in favour of the landlords and it was even more attractive than the prevailing system. The campaign conducted against the old agrarian system, and sharecropping, as one of its main elements at the beginning of the land reform, might have acclerated the switch over to the fixed-rent tenancy.

Division of the land between peasants and landlords which comprised only 10 per cent of all cases in the whole country, was the second popular choice among landlords (see Table 6.5). This option was widely chosen in Fars where 44 per cent of the peasants received a share of the land. Fars alone was responsible for about half of all cases which were settled by division in the whole country. The main reason for this was probably that the landlords generally received a larger share than the peasants in this region; in many cases, their share was three-quarters or four-fifths of the crop (Lambton 1969: 242). Where land was settled by division, landlords retained the most fertile part of it and sometimes occupied more land than they were actually entitled to since there was no cadastral survey and many land reform officials worked in favour of the landowners. A large number of the peasants who received land by division ended up with a plot of land that was too small to provide them with a living and were therefore dissatisfied (see Lambton 1969: 242–9; OIPFG 1973: 56–9).

A small number of the peasants, 4 per cent, received land from their landlords who selected option (2). On the other hand, about one per cent of the peasants lost their land as the landlords managed to 'persuade' them to sell their cultivation rights. The available evidence indicates that not all such peasants sold their rights of their own free will. Some were forced by the landlords and some others were deceived by their landlords and signed the documents of sale without knowing what they were doing (see Lambton 1969: 253–5; OIPFG 1973: 60–3; Azkia 1986: 115–16). However, the great majority of the peasants who sold their rights, i.e. 79 per cent, were from Kerman and Khorasan.

According to the official statistics (see Table 6.5) 57,164 peasants bought the land that they had been cultivating and 156,279 peasants received only part of the land they used to cultivate. Thus, about 213,500 peasant families received some land in the second stage. Meanwhile, 23,401 peasants 'sold' their traditional rights and became landless. The number of peasants who became landless may certainly have been higher since there were landlords who deprived the peasants of their traditional rights by declaring their land mechanized or by other methods.[20] We should remember that a) more than 70 per cent of the peasants who received land obtained only small plots of land through the division option, and b) in addition to the likely exaggeration in the number of beneficiaries, which was revealed earlier in the case of the first stage, some of the beneficiaries of the second stage had already received land in the first stage and, therefore, the above number also contains some double-counting in this respect.[21]

We have no information about the amount of land which was distributed in the second stage. If we assume that a) the peasants who received land by division, obtained on average one-third of the land that they had been cultivating, and b) every fifty families who received land, represent one six-*dang* village, we find that the distributed land in the second stage was approximately equivalent to 2,185 entire villages. The first assumption is based on the fact, mentioned above, that land division occurred mainly in places where crop division was generally in favour of landowners, e.g. in Fars. The second assumption relies on the official data which show that the average population of the Iranian villages is fifty households. We have thus overlooked the fact that we could assume that seventy-five peasants represent one village according to the inflated official statistics (see p. 95).

In sum, about 4 per cent of all Iranian villages were distributed as a result of the second stage of land reform among 7 per cent of the rural families. This slow-down in the land redistribution programme underlines the pro-landlord nature of the second stage, especially in comparison with the initial period of the first stage.

The third stage of land reform

The second stage of land reform turned 1,246,652 sharecroppers into fixed-rent tenants while the situation of 83,267 peasants who were in the owner–peasant joint stock corporations remained unchanged (see Table 6.5). Moreover, 172,103 peasants who share-cropped the endowed land (*vaqf*) received 99-year tenancy contracts according to the provisions of the law of the second stage (see Hooglund 1982: 65, Table 3). The third stage of land reform which was introduced in January 1969 should be seen in relation to the deep sense of dissatisfaction of these 1.5 million peasants (see Hooglund 1982: 67–9 and Momeni 1980: 239–41). Accordingly, all the rented land, except *vaqf* land, as well as the land of owner-peasant corporations were either to be sold to the peasants or to be divided between the two parties in proportion to their traditional share of the crop.

Although the law was passed at the beginning of 1969, its implementation progressed very slowly. If we assume that all eligible landlords were those given for 1973 in Table 6.6, i.e. 342,000, only one-third of them had declared their intention to sell or divide their estates by May 1971 (see Denman 1973: 149, Table 12). Table 6.6 is convincing evidence that the total number of landlords who actually sold or divided their land must have been much lower. We can also see that as late as March 1972, i.e. six months after the reform had officially been terminated, only 45 per cent of all the eligible landlords had transferred their land, or part of it, to the peasants.

Table 6.6 Implementation of the third stage of land reform

	March 1972	March 1973
Sale:		
(i) Landlords who agreed to sell	281,470	305,000
(ii) Landlords who actually sold	144,219	229,000
(iii) Beneficiaries	564,203	842,000
Division:		
(i) Landlords who agreed to divide	41,221	37,000
(ii) Landlords who actually divided	10,129	24,000
(iii) Beneficiaries	32,031	75,000

Source: Bank Markazi Iran, *Annual Report and Balance Sheet* (1972–3)

Several reasons have been given for the sluggish progress of the final stage of land reform. Hooglund argues that the government did little to implement the third stage. The government avoided taking part in the process of transferring ownership or educating the peasants about the law and, instead, tried to persuade the owners to sell voluntarily to the peasants (Hooglund 1982: 69–71). Denman, on the other hand, maintains that landowners and their tenants preferred different methods of settlement and this resulted in a delay in the implementation of the third stage (Denman 1973: 145–6). This argument is based on the result of an inquiry about the preferences of landlords which was carried out at the beginning of the third stage. It showed that 88 per cent of the 222,360 who answered the inquiry preferred land division (Denman 1973: 145–6). However, such differences could not have had considerable effects on the progress of the third stage, according to the law, it was the landlords who were able to select the option they wanted. Moreover, the pro-landlord attitude of the government would have enabled the landlords to conclude 'agreements' with their tenants at their own convenience (see Chapter 5, pp. 81–3; also Hooglund 1982: 70).

However, we can see from Table 6.6 that there might have been a sudden increase in land reform activities after 1972. Other official statistics indicate that the implementation of the third stage must have been completed by 1974. Accordingly, all the small landowners covered by the law either sold their lands to 1,154,578 tenants or chose the division option and transferred part of their land to 110,347 farmers (Statistical Centre of Iran 1976: 212–13). This means that 1,264,925 peasants might have received land under the third stage.

There are grounds for questioning the reliability of these data. First, most eligible landowners seem to have preferred division to sale (see OIPFG 1973: 68 and Momeni 1982: 258).[22] The official statistics show the opposite. The figures for the last year might have also been inflated to take account of the wishes of the authorities who wanted to bring the land reform to a close.

An estimate must now be provided for the number of villages that were distributed during this stage. The estimate, however, cannot be based on 1,264,925 peasants who received land under the third stage since many of them were not first-time beneficiaries. Salmanzadeh and Jones (1979: 121) have shown that about 35 per cent of all beneficiaries of the third stage in 169 villages had already received land in the first stage. It is then likely that 842,283 farmers – two-thirds of the total – were first-time beneficiaries of this stage (cf. Majd 1987). Provided that, once more, fifty peasants represent

101

one entire village, and ignoring that in the division cases tenants received only part of the rented land, the redistributed land might have been equivalent to about 16,866 villages.[23]

This figure is a remarkable result because it constitutes about 28 per cent of all Iranian villages and is higher than the result of the first stage. However, a comparison between the number of affected landowners and peasants in Table 6.6 indicates that these villages were in general the property of small landowners. Moreover, a large part of the redistributed lands were probably in less fertile regions, since the landed properties of most small landowners were located in such regions.[24]

Apart from the lands redistributed under different stages of the reform, some land was also distributed among peasants as a result of the law of transfer of ownership of endowed lands (*vaqfs*) to tenants, which was passed in 1971. We will assume that all 172,103 tenants of these lands received the ownership of the tenanted farms (see p. 100).[25]

The distribution of land ownership and land tenure after the reform

Table 6.7 summarizes our discussion about the results of the land redistribution in Iran after 1962. In respect of the number of beneficiaries, the results of the reform appear to be very impressive: 92 per cent of eligible families received land after 1962. Moreover, redistribution of state domains and crown estates which had begun before 1962 gave another 157,000 peasants the ownership of 2,676 whole villages (4 per cent of all villages).[26] This implies that by the end of the land reform *all* sharecroppers and fixed-rent tenants must have become peasant proprietors.

In reality, however, progress was certainly not as impressive as on paper. We have already shown that the official figures are highly exaggerated. Furthermore, some cultivators 'sold' their cultivation rights during the second stage and some others also lost their rights in one way or another. Finally, there were tenants who continued to cultivate the landlords' land in the same manner as they had done before the reform.[27] All in all, we can conclude that land reform succeeded in giving land to a large majority of the eligible peasants while most of the remainder lost their rights and joined the landless labourers.

In sum, our relatively generous estimates indicate that about 60 per cent of all villages were redistributed among peasants. This, however, in no way means that 60 per cent of the agricultural land was transferred to the beneficiaries. Village lands varied greatly in

Table 6.7 Results of the Iranian land reform, 1962−75

	Beneficiaries		Redistributed land (village equivalent)	
	No. of families	% of eligible families	No.	% of all villages
First stage	709,718	34	9,514	16
Second stage	213,443	10	2,185	4
Third stage	843,283	40	16,866	28
Vaqf land	172,103	8	3,442	6
Total	1,938,547	92	32,007	53

Note: a This is assumed to be equal to the number of families with cultivation rights, i.e. approximately 70 per cent of rural families who were potentially eligible to receive land.

size and soil quality. The villages of the large landlords tended to be located in more fertile regions and they were usually the larger ones (see Chapter 3, pp. 30−1).[28] It was also the large landowners who might have retained a large proportion of their landed properties. Considering the fact that the large landowners were principally affected by the first stage, Table 6.7 suggests that most of the redistributed land might have belonged to small landowners (cf. Momeni 1980: 266 and Hooglund 1982: 79). It is thus plausible to believe that the 40 per cent of villages which remained in the hands of landowners were among the more fertile and larger ones. This implies that landowners, especially the large ones, might have owned at least half of the agricultural land after the reform.

It is not then surprising that a large majority of peasants received only small plots of land which in many cases were probably less than the holdings they used to cultivate. In some cases, for example, when part of a village was redistributed in the first stage, all the peasants who had cultivation rights on the entire land of the village shared that part and, therefore, ended up with smaller farms than before (OIPFG 1973: 45). This was also true for the land divided between peasants and landlords under the second and third stages. We can imagine the size of this group of peasants if we look at the numbers of such peasants in Tables 6.3, 6.5, and 6.6. At the same time, a minority received proportionately larger and more fertile farms. These people were generally former village-headmen and *buneh* leaders (Hooglund 1982: 89; Azkia 1986: 126−7; Lambton 1969: 177). Consequently, while many peasants received less than 3 hectares, few received as much as 50 hectares or even more. Different studies suggest that the holdings of the majority of the land reform beneficiaries might have been between 0.5 and 10 hectares.[29]

Most of the estimates on landownership after the reform are based on statistics which show peasant holdings, i.e. data similar to those in Table 6.8. For instance a study assumes, on the basis of personal observation, that all holdings over 20 hectares, which constituted about 50 per cent of the crop land, belonged to approximately 200,000 absentee landowners (Hooglund 1982: 78−9).[30] In view of the fact that some landowners had divided their land into holdings of different sizes and nominally transferred them to their relatives and friends, there must have been owners who possessed several holdings (see Bavandi 1982: 90; Hooglund 1982: 91, Table 5; Khosrovi 1981: 30). This implies that landownership was more skewed than can be inferred from such data. Some information which has come out recently reveals that there were landowners in Gorgan and Khorasan who had more than 10,000 hectares each. The names of nine landlords who owned between 2,000 and 9,000 hectares have also been published (*Ettela'at* 1980, cited in Azkia 1980: 64; *Ettela'at* 1986: 11).

The large, and medium, landowners who were comparatively very small in number still owned almost half of the agricultural land while the other half belonged to about 2 million farmers. A large majority of these farmers became owners as a result of the redistribution of part of the land of large landlords and a major part of the land of small landowners.

Some of the landowners continued to lease out their land, or part of it, for a fixed rent or a share of the crop even after the reform. However, the post-reform tenancy and sharecropping systems were not always similar to those of the pre-reform era. The tenants and sharecroppers did not have any special rights to the land. They cultivated the land for a specific period of time, e.g. for six months, and the contract might or might not be extended when it expired (see Momeni 1980: 342; Antoun 1981: 226). Moreover, not only the landlords but also small peasants might lease out their lands. Such small peasants earned their living as workers or construction labourers in the cities and therefore had to let their lands. The tenants could be well-to-do and competent farmers who came from other regions, especially from Yazd on the borders of the central desert. They cultivated summer crops and vegetables and might leave the village after the harvest (Azkia 1980: 113). Different types of sharecropping also developed after the reform.

Pump cultivation was one type of share tenancy which became common after the reform. In this sytem, tenants dug a well in non-irrigated, and sometimes uncultivated, land and installed water pumps on them. They used modern techniques to cultivate the land and paid one-tenth of the crop to the landowner (Ashraf and Banuazizi 1980: 38−9; Azkia 1980: 116−17).[31]

Official statistics show, for example, that 2 per cent of all peasants were tenants who cultivated about 3 per cent of the farm-land around 1975 (Khosrovi 1981: 27–30). If sharecropping, tenant–owner cultivation, and other types of tenancies are taken into account, it could be said that the tenanted land might have accounted for about 10 per cent of the cultivated land (Bavandi 1982: 88; see also Khosrovi 1982: 25–43).

The above statistics indicate that the tenants were distributed among all different sizes of holdings but they were concentrated in the holdings which were less than five hectares (Khosrovi 1981: 30). This means that most tenants were small farmers and might have experienced little change after the reform. Case studies show that this was true for a lot of peasants who still sharecropped under the traditional conditions (Momeni 1980: 338–41).

In spite of the presence of the traditional and new types of tenancy after the reform, the significance of tenancy has consider-ably diminished. On the other hand, peasant proprietorship and large, modern estates which were uncommon before the reform became the predominant type of tenure as the result of the land reform.

Although most peasants owned the lands they cultivated, a large majority of them had to eke out their livelihood from a small plot of land. At the same time, most former landlords stopped renting their lands, which was common before the reform. The general tendency among them was to form large, and/or medium farms, under their direct or indirect management. These farms, although small in number, covered most of the cultivated land. This is clearly illustrated in Table 6.8. We should remember that the classification of all farms in different regions of Iran on the basis of the same size criteria may involve some overgeneralization. There is in fact a great deal of regional variation. For example, in Gilan, where agricultural conditions are very favourable and farms are normally small, farms of 20 to 30 hectares could be considered as large farms. On the other hand, in Sistan and Baluchestan with detri-mental conditions even 10–20 hectare farms display the charac-teristics of small farms (cf. Khosrovi 1981: 11–12). However, such differences are within certain limits and do not materially affect the general picture which is provided by Table 6.8.

We should note that the farm categories shown in Table 6.8 do not necessarily correspond to different farmer groups, i.e. small, medium and large farmers. These were very likely large farmers who owned, for example, several medium-sized farms. In order to better understand the post-reform agrarian system and develop-ments we should examine large and small farmers in more detail.

Table 6.8   Distribution of land holdings by size, 1974

Size of holding (hectares)	Number	% of total number	Area (hectares)	% of total area
Small				
<2	1,056,467	43	703,562	4
2– 5	541,592	22	1,732,868	11
5–10	427,934	17	2,953,447	18
Medium				
10–20	304,000	12	4,487,000	27
20–30	97,000	4	1,904,000	12
Large				
30–50	27,074	1	1,109,741	7
>50	25,822	1	3,526,603	21
Total	2,479,989	100	16,417,221	100

Source: Khosrovi (1981: 57; 1982: 13–14)

Large farmers

According to our classification, farms of 30 hectares or more should be considered as large farms. But there is not a general agreement about this. For example, some assume that farms of 50 or more hectares were large farms while others maintain that farms which were as large as 100 hectares or more were truly large-scale holdings (for instance, see Khosrovi 1981: 41–5; Azkia 1986: 120–1; Hooglund 1982: 82–3; and Aresvik 1976: 100–1). We have included 30–50 hectare farms among large farms for several reasons. First of all, we are interested in the land concentration phenomenon which causes market imperfections and this small group also possessed a proportionately high percentage of the land. Second, farms between 10 and 50 hectares are usually assumed to be medium farms whose owners are rich by Iranian standards (see, among others, Khosrovi 1982: 41–4 and Azkia 1986: 126–7). Accordingly, farms of 30–50 hectares land are generally considered to be upper-medium and their owners are among the richest peasants who enjoy more power than the majority. These farmers are then very close to those commonly called large owners and our assumption does not differ significantly from many others. Finally, there is evidence which shows that from the point of view of land and water, these farms were in a radically better position than those which were less than 30 hectares (Khosrovi 1982: 42).[32]

On the whole, large farms consisted of three types of farms: individual large farms, agribusinesses, and farm corporations. The first kind of large farms were the dominant form of large-scale holdings and covered more than 85 per cent of all the land which belonged to such farms. It is interesting to note that large farms of 100 hectares and above comprised only 18 per cent of these farms but occupied more than 50 per cent of their land (see Khosrovi 1981: 57, Table 9). Although many large farmers were former large and medium landowners, other social groups could also be found among them; for example, merchants, military officers, former village headmen, etc. A large number of large holdings were concentrated in Gorgan, Khorasan and Khuzestan which are among the very fertile regions (Hooglund 1982: 83; Azkia 1986: 121). In fact, even other large farms were concentrated mainly in the more fertile regions of the country.[33] We should remember that some of the large farmers owned several holdings which were either large or small, or both. This implies that large farmers must have controlled much more land than large farms cover, i.e. 28 per cent as shown in Table 6.8.

Agribusinesses emerged as a result of the law of 1968 which encouraged the establishment of large and modern estates on the land irrigated by dams (see Chapter 5, pp. 83–5). By 1978, thirty-seven agribusinesses had been established on 238,000 hectares of irrigated land (Azkia 1980: 128). Fifteen of these farms were very large estates, i.e. between 5,000 to 25,000 hectares, and controlled by multinational companies, while the remaining twenty-two agri-businesses were smaller, i.e. 1,000–5,000 hectares, and belonged to Iranian shareholders (Azkia 1980: 128).[34] In some cases, the government forced the peasants to sell their land to make way for agribusinesses. For example, it is estimated that about 55,000 peasants must have 'sold' their land to the government which leased it for thirty years to eleven large agribusinesses. It is therefore plausible to believe that at least 75,000 peasants were displaced for the establishment of the thirty-seven agribusinesses (Azkia 1980: 129; Hooglund 1982: 85; Momeni 1980: 358).

The third type of large holdings were farm corporations. They were created in accordance with the 1967 law which governed their establishment. Only four months after the law was passed, the first corporation was established and the number of such farms increased to ninety-four by 1978. These corporations were spread over the whole country but they were mostly established in the more fertile regions and on lands downstream of dams. They tended to be close to towns which means that they usually enjoyed good communication facilities as well. Each farm corporation, on the average comprised between eight and ten villages and all ninety-four corporations encompassed 850 villages which covered about 400,000 hectares. These farm corporations had more than 35,000 shareholders and covered about 300,000 villagers (Denman 1973: 213–15; Momeni 1980: 359–63; Hooglund 1982: 86–7; Azkia 1986: 235).[35]

It might be argued that the farm corporations differed from other large farms in the sense that they were controlled by a large number of shareholders rather than a few people. Moreover, the shareholders consisted of both large landowners and peasants who had one vote each irrespective of the number of shares they hold.[36] In practice, however, it was principally the large shareholders who occupied the key positions in farm corporations, such as on the board of directors (see Azkia 1986: 237 and Momeni 1980: 366). Moreover, the managing directors and their expert assistants, who were nominated civil servants, conducted the corporations like large landowners. They seldom consulted even the board of directors (Momeni 1980: 366–7; Group of Experts 1980: 41–4). It is therefore not unreasonable to assume that the corporations were also large farms under the control of a handful of people.

Small farmers

On average, an Iranian farmer has to have about 7 hectares to be able to support his family (see Hooglund 1982: 77 and Momeni 1980: 70–1). This might be enough to explain why farmers with less than 10 hectares are widely assumed to be small farmers. Most of these farmers have received land under different stages of the land reform. Ignoring the fact that some of the small farms belonged to others and were rented by their cultivators, we can assume that the number of small farmers was approximately equivalent to that of the small farms shown in Table 6.8.

As Table 6.8 illustrates, the land distribution was very unequal among the small farmers. More than 50 per cent of all the small peasants possessed holdings which were less than 2 hectares, i.e. their farms were much smaller than the size which was necessary for basic subsistence (see Table 6.8). Even those peasants of this group whose lands were in Gilan where there was abundant rainfall could not rely solely on their farms for their living and had to work for others as well (see Khosrovi 1981: 141–3). It was in fact quite common that at least one of the family members of the small peasants worked for medium and large farmers or as casual labourers in the cities (see Khosrovi 1979: 81–3; Azkia 1986: 124; and Lambton 1969: 146).

A large majority of the peasants who owned between 2 and 5 hectares were normally in the same situation as the owners of the mini-holdings. Only a small number of such peasants who cultivated rice, vegetables and summer crops were better off than the others (Khosrovi 1981: 34). In other words, from Table 6.8 we can say that 65 per cent of all farmers in Iran, or about 80 per cent of the small peasants, had to work more or less outside their farms in order to earn their living.

The smallness of farms was not the only problem which faced the small farmers. Irrigation difficulties and land fragmentation were two other factors which affected them adversely.

We know from Chapter 3 that before the reform peasant holdings consisted of several separate plots of varying quality. Since the reform transferred to the peasants the land that they were cultivating before the reform, their farms remained fragmented even after the reform. To the extent that the peasants received all the land of their village and its water resources, the reform did not aggravate the old water and land fragmentation problems. In some cases, such beneficiaries could even improve their irrigation systems immediately after the reform (Lambton 1969: 288).

The situation was, however, quite different in partially redistributed villages. We observed in the previous sections that the landlords retained the best lands and sold the poorest lands to the peasants. The small peasants had to reallocate their share of land which was again divided into small plots. Consequently, the lands of these peasants also consisted of scattered plots while their holdings diminished in size. Furthermore, the landowners controlled water resources in such villages and allocated a much larger proportion of the village water to their own large holdings. If we recall that most of the villages were only partially redistributed, it is reasonable to assume that irrigation and land fragmentation problems became more serious for a large majority of the peasants (see Khosrovi 1979b: 165–9; Hooglund 1982: 90–1).[37]

Concluding remarks

The Iranian land reform succeeded in redistributing, at best, about 50 per cent of the agricultural land among the farmers. A large amount of the redistributed land belonged to the small landowners. Large landed properties were in fact affected mainly by the first stage of the land reform, especially in the early phase of the reform when the law was enforced rather vigorously. However, even then, the large landowners evaded the law and took full advantage of its loopholes. They managed to retain a great part of their land. This was the best land with easy access to water sources in the majority of the affected villages. On the whole, a small group of people still controlled a large proportion of the land and water sources.

Agriculture, poverty and reform in Iran

Large owners generally took over their land rather than leasing it to others, which was a common practice in the pre-reform era. There was an increasing tendency among this group to form large and/or medium-sized farms and cultivate them under their direct or indirect management. This was the main reason for the sharp increase in the number of large farms and the land they occupied. Part of the increase in the number and size of the large farms might have resulted from bringing new land under cultivation. At the same time, the number of very small farms grew rather quickly as well. However, the increase of the landholdings of such farms fell far behind the increase in their number. The transfer to the peasants of only part of their rights to land might have been the principal reason for this process.

Table 6.9 summarizes the changes which took place in the structure of the Iranian landholding system after the reform. It illustrates that although the total number of farms and the area under cultivation increased rather quickly after the land reform, it was the large farms which increased most of all. In fact, the largest farms tended to become both more numerous and larger. On the other hand, we can see from Table 6.9 that the number of small farms increased relative to their area. This implies that the small farms also grew in number but they generally became smaller.

Table 6.9 Growth of holdings and their area, 1960–74 (percentage)

Size (hectares)	Number	Area
<2	41	23
2– 5	14	12
5–10	26	22
10–20	36	49
20–50	60	36
>50	106	127
Total	32	45

Sources: FAO (1966: 96–7); Table 6.8

We can reasonably argue that the traditional agrarian system moved toward a bimodal system as the result of the reform. However, did the difference between the size of the land which was owned and cultivated by the large landowners and small peasants really spread to credit and labour markets? Was there any difference between the two types of farms with respect to their methods of cultivation, the crops they grew, etc.? We will try to answer these and other related questions in the next chapter.

110

Chapter seven

Economic consequences of the land reform

We saw in the previous chapter that the concentration of land in a few hands persisted in post-reform Iran. However, in contrast to pre-reform Iran, the large landowners tended to become 'large farmers'. That is to say, they increasingly formed large and medium-sized farms under their own management. A large majority of former tenants constituted the numerous group of 'small farmers' as they received some land under different stages of the land reform. In other words, it appears that the traditional tenancy system became transformed into a bimodal system after the reform.

The analysis of Chapter 4 concluded that large farmers in such a system not only have more land but also have easier access to capital. Small farmers, on the other hand, have relatively more labour at their disposal. Hence the conditions prevailing in the factor markets are not the same for all farmers. This in turn causes inefficient allocation of resources. Moreover, the two groups of farmers who face different factor prices would exhibit different patterns of economic behaviour. While large farmers will tend to use modern technology and inputs and will increasingly cultivate cash crops, peasants will be confined to traditional methods of production and the cultivation of subsistence crops. Government policies in a bimodal system are normally in favour of large farmers which will strengthen the above tendencies.

In the present chapter, we want to examine the Iranian bimodal system in order to find out if large and small farmers really faced different conditions in factor markets other than land, and if there were growing contrasts between the two groups of farmers as the theory suggests. We will also study the outcome of the government's policies for each group. Finally, we will try to see how the post-reform changes affected agricultural growth in Iran. But, in view of the importance of irrigation in Iranian agriculture, we should perhaps begin with an examination of the impact of the land reform on the accessibility of irrigation water to different groups of farmers before turning to the other issues.

The land reform and irrigation sources

Access to water sources became more difficult for the peasants after the land reform for several reasons. First, the law allowed the landowners to choose the land they wanted to retain and they chose the best land with good water resources. This was especially common where only part of the village land was transferred to the peasants. In these villages, peasants received plots of land which were often far from the water supply. If such villages depended on *qanats* or wells for irrigation they generally remained in the hands of the landowners although, according to the law, the irrigated land had to be transferred to the peasants inclusive of its water rights (see Azkia 1980: 112; Hooglund 1982: 91–2; for some examples see OIPFG 1974).

Apart from retaining the title to source of water supply, landlords exercised other practices which limited irrigation opportunities for the peasants. In many cases, the landlords reallocated the irrigation water so that their retained land received more water than they were legally entitled to. One way, for instance, was to change the rotation of water. Let us assume that the peasant farms had the right to water once in eight days. The rotation could then be increased so that the peasants would only get water once in, say, fifteen days (Lambton 1969: 284–7; see also OIPG 1974).

Landowners were sometimes alleged to demand high prices for irrigation water. There were cases where many peasants felt that they were unable to pay water charges and began to rely exclusively on the uncertainties of rain, or to leave increasingly more of their land fallow every year, or to rent out part of it to the larger owners (Hooglund 1982: 92–3).

The second reason that facilitated irrigation for the larger farmers, and which probably adversely affected the peasants, was the development of power-operated wells. Large farmers were able to invest in power-operated, deep and semi-deep wells, something which peasants normally could not afford. This type of investment which began before the reform increased markedly afterwards (see, for example, Momeni 1980: 326). It is believed that the sinking of deep wells was in part responsible for the reduction of water to some *qanats* which irrigated the peasants' farms in several regions (Lambton 1969: 289–90; Momeni 1980: 399; OIPFG 1974: 2).

Finally, the government's irrigation policies and projects were much more beneficial to large farmers than to the peasants; they were sometimes prohibitive for the latter. For example, the Ministry of Water and Power abolished customary water rights which existed in parts of Azarbayjan and demanded water dues from the farmers. The peasants complained that water was sold to the highest bidder or that they had to pay high water dues although they grew only grain crops which used little water in comparison to cash crops (Lambton 1969: 278–9).

The government correctly considered the scarcity of water to be a major problem for Iranian agriculture and gave priority to irrigation projects in its agricultural investments. For instance, irrigation projects absorbed about 45 per cent of total government expenditure in agriculture between 1963 and 1972 (Bank Markazi Iran, *Annual Report and Balance Sheet* 1965–1975). However, most of the government outlay for irrigation was allocated to the construction of big dams and water networks which yielded little benefit to the peasants. As we saw in the previous chapter, the land under the dams was allocated to agribusinesses and farm corporations.[1] These dams might reduce the flow of water in the streams that were used by the peasants or even dry them up, something which happened in Sistan (Momeni 1980: 397–8). Where peasants had access to the water of these dams, they had to pay more than agribusiness for the water: each cubic metre of the irrigation water cost the peasants 0.15 rials while the agribusiness companies paid 0.12 rials for it (Azkia 1980: 127; Dumont 1978: 17).

In sum, sources of water supply were under the control of the larger farmers, which normally meant that they had easier access to water than peasants. The government's irrigation policies often reinforced the prevailing situation. We should note that the unequal access to water implies that if land is measured in efficiency units, the extent of land concentration will in fact be greater than shown by the crude measures of land area such as numbers of hectares.[2]

The rural capital market

The borrowing conditions in the rural capital market were not the same for the two groups of farmers. First and foremost, large farmers were among the richest in the society and in all probability had large savings. They could draw from them whenever they needed money. Most of the peasants, on the other hand, were in debt when they received their land. While it is impossible to prove the former assertion, our discussion in Chapter 3 substantiates the latter (see pp. 44–7). Moreover, the peasants were principally land reform beneficiaries and had to pay, in fifteen years, the instalments of the land they received.

For their financial needs, farmers could borrow from commercial banks, the government or the informal credit market. The Iranian commercial banks provided about 20 per cent of the agricultural credit between 1963 and 1973 (see Table 7.1). The difficulties involved in obtaining loans from commercial banks, such as the necessity of providing security or finding a guarantor, deprived the peasants of borrowing from these sources (Khosrovi 1979b: 160). It was then principally large farmers, processors, merchants and exporters who received most of the agricultural loans from these banks (Aresvik 1976: 171).

As Table 7.1 shows, more than 60 per cent of the institutional credits of the agricultural sector consisted of state loans. These loans were given to farmers through co-operative societies, the Agricultural Bank (the Agricultural Co-operative Bank of Iran), the Agricultural Development Bank of Iran, and some special government agencies.[3]

Table 7.1 Relative importance of various sources of agricultural credit, 1963–72 (estimated average)

Source of credit	Amount (billion rials)	%
Agricultural Co-operative Bank	9.0	14
Agricultural Development Bank	0.4	1
Commercial banks	13.2	20
Government agencies	5.1	8
Rural co-operatives	6	9
Non-institutional sources	32.3	49
Total	66	100

Source: Aresvik (1976: 169)

Rural co-operative societies were in practice the most accessible source of institutional credit available to peasants. These co-operatives were supposed to cover all the land reform beneficiaries. According to the provisions of the first stage, the eligible peasants received land if they were members of rural co-operative societies (see Chapter 5, pp. 85–6). The number of co-operatives, however, increased slowly. There had been 8,361 co-operatives serving about 30,000 villages by the end of 1972 (Statistical Centre of Iran 1976: 215). Some of these co-operatives existed only on paper and about half of the villages can be said not to have had co-operative societies. In 1972, it was decided to consolidate the societies and consequently their number decreased to 2,717 in 1973 (Statistical Centre of Iran 1976: 215). As a result, the members of 6,000 dissolved co-operatives had to rely on the bigger co-operatives which were located in larger villages. In some cases, for example, peasants in twenty different villages were members of one and the same society (Hooglund 1982: 106). Considering the dispersion of villages in Iran and the communication difficulties, this might in practice have deprived some members of the benefits of the societies. This may partly explain the bitterness and objections of the members of smaller co-operatives toward such a plan from its early beginning (see Denman 1973: 202).

The major activity of the co-operatives was to provide loans to their members. The loans were principally financed by the Agricultural Bank and a small share of them was provided out of the co-operatives' own capital and reserves. But these sources were not enough to meet peasants' credit needs and therefore co-operative loans comprised on average only 9 per cent of agricultural credit between 1963 and 1972 (See Table 7.1). The loans which were granted by the societies were principally short-term. For instance, in the period 1965 to 1972 more than 90 per cent of the loans granted by the societies were for 6 to 12 months (Azakia 1980: 98; see also Hooglund 1982: 110).

The amounts of most of the loans were also low. While the average expenditure for producing 1 hectare of dry-farmed winter wheat was about 6,000 rials, the average co-operative loans hardly exceeded this amount during the period 1963 to 1971. The amount of loans increased rapidly after 1971 but, considering the peasants' needs and inflation, such increases were insignificant. For example, loans per head in 1972–3 show an increase of 25 per cent over 1970–1 while the inflation rate for the same period was about 20 per cent (see Table 7.3 and Bank Markazi Iran, *Bulletin* 1975).[4] Moreover, co-operatives were not even able to provide such limited loans to all their members: between 1963 and 1973, only 55 per cent of the total members received co-operative loans (Statistical Centre of Iran 1975: 183, 211; 1976: 184, 215). This figure is certainly an overestimate since it was quite common to grant a 'new' loan to the peasant who could not repay his previous loan and take the new loan as payment for the old one (see Katouzian 1974: 233).

There is also evidence which indicates that the richer members of the societies had easier access to co-operative loans than the poorer ones. First, the amount of the loan was related to the number of shares owned by each member. Each member could borrow up to ten times the value of his shares, but in no case more than 20,000 rials (Hooglund 1982: 109; Azukia 1980: 280). Second, it was the manager of each society who in practice decided about the loans. In most of the co-operatives the more prosperous farmers occupied such positions, especially after the consolidation of the co-operatives, and the abuse of power, for example to ensure more credit for themselves, their friends, etc., was a widespread practice among them (see Azkia 1980: 280–1; Hooglund 1982: 106; Lambton 1969: 337–8).

Small farmers could also borrow money from the Agricultural Bank. However, about 65 per cent of the loans from this source were granted to members of co-operatives through the societies and only 5 per cent were directly lent to the members as individuals. Around 25 per cent of loans were given to non-members and 5 per cent to supervised credit projects (Aresvik 1976: 171–2).

Table 7.2 illustrates some basic features of the loans that were granted by the Agricultural Bank between 1963 and 1973. It can be seen that most of the loans of the bank were small and short-term. Table 7.2 also shows that the percentage of loans which were below 10,000 rials decreased while that between 10,000 and 50,000 increased. In other words, the size of the loans tended to increase during this period. However, the facts that the Agricultural Bank mainly paid loans to peasants via the co-operative societies and that the average loan of the co-operatives was close to 10,000 rials may imply that the smaller loans were much more frequent in the group of 10,000–50,000 rials. In accordance with co-operative loans, a large majority of small loans were in all probability short-term.

Moreover, Table 7.2 indicates that 93 to 98 per cent of the loans of the Agricultural Bank amounted to less than 50,000 rials. But the available information indicates that the loans which were more than 50,000, although small in numbers, absorbed a large proportion of the credits. Between 1965 and 1969, for example, about 36 per cent of the total credits of the bank was allocated to such loans (Statistical Centre of Iran 1976: 183; Bank Markazi Iran, *Annual Report and Balance Sheet* 1970: 126). Considering the percentages of short-term loans (Table 7.2) and the fact that a great majority of them were in fact co-operative loans it is reasonable to conclude that most of the large loans might have been medium- and long-term.

On the whole, we can divide credits which were provided by the Agricultural Bank into two groups: (a) small, short-term loans which were mostly given to peasants through co-operatives and (b) large, medium- and long-term loans which were given directly to farmers. Small farmers were in practice deprived of the latter loans. First and foremost, the granting and the size of loans was closely related to the collateral offered by the borrowers (Aresvik 1976:

172). Small farmers could hardly provide such a security, especially for larger loans. Moreover, the branches of the bank were in large towns. Regarding detailed security requirements, paperwork and delays, it sometimes took a week or more to process a loan. During this period, the peasants had to stay in towns, or if possible, travel there several times. In each case, the costs of getting loans to peasants were certainly prohibitive (see Aresvik 1976: 174; Katouzian 1974: 234; Momeni 1980: 405).

Table 7.2   Credit allocated by the Agricultural Bank, 1963−73

	1963−7	1968−9	1970−1	1972−3
Total number (thousands)	2,048	675	445	609
Total amount (million rials)	23,394	10,705	18,491	34,374
% of loans < 10,000 rials	76[a]	69	62	34
% of loans 10,000−50,000 rials	20[a]	29	32	59
% of total amount of short-term loans[c]	49	63	83[b]	75[b]

Sources: Statistical Centre of Iran (1975, 1976) and Bank Markazi Iran, *Annual Report and Balance Sheet*, (1971, 1973, 1974)

Notes: a For 1966−7
b The figures stand for only one year in each group, i.e. 1971 and 1973
c Up to two years

Large long-term loans were also provided by the Agricultural Development Bank. This bank was founded to finance the development of large farms. The bank normally lent to farmers with holdings in excess of 500 hectares. However, farmers with farms as 'small' as 100 hectares also had access to its loans. The minimum loan was one million rials and the bank could lend up to 80 per cent of investment outlays. Its only borrowers were naturally large farms such as farm corporations and agribusinesses (Aresvik 1976: 172; Katouzian 1983: 333).

In general, it can be said that peasants only had access to institutional credits only through the co-operatives while the large farmers were able to borrow both from the Agricultural Bank and from the Agricultural Development Bank.[5] Table 7.3 shows that the average loan varied greatly from source to source. The co-operatives gave the smallest loans per capita. It should be noted that if we could eliminate the negative effect of the small co-operative loans which are included in the loans of the Agricultural Bank, the difference in the average loan available from these sources would become much larger.

Unequal access to government credits was in fact the natural outcome of the government's general agricultural policy. The analysis of agricultural policies in Chapter 5 showed that they generally supported large farmers. It was also as a result of such a policy that the government granted large sums of money to farm corporations or provided agribusinesses access to road and drainage facilities, etc. free of charge (see Denman 1978: 287; Azkia 1980: 126–7; Bagley 1976: 30). The privileges of farm corporations are clearly evident in Table 7.4. It illustrates that each peasant who borrowed through co-operatives in the period 1968 to 1971 received, on average, loans which were only 11 to 18 per cent of the loans and grants per shareholder received by corporations in the same period. Moreover, more than 70 per cent of the sums which corporations received were in fact grants. It should be also noted that corporation loans received were in fact grants. It should be also noted that corporation loans were medium- and long-term with an effective interest rate of one per cent. The interest rate of co-operative loans was 6 per cent.[6]

Table 7.3   Average state loans per recipient by source of credit, 1968–74 (thousand rials)

Source	1968–9	1970–1	1972–3	1974
Cooperatives[a]	6,800	7,400	9,300	14,500
Agricultural Bank	15,200	41,600	56,400	n.a.
Agricultural Development Bank[b]	18,600	20,500	8,900	29,500

Sources: Bank Markazi Iran, *Annual Report and Balance Sheet* (1971–5); Statistical Centre of Iran (1976)

Notes: a A small part of co-operative loans was financed by their own capital and reserves
b The figures are loan and government participation per project

Table 7.4   State loans and grants to co-operative societies and farm corporations, 1968–71 (rials per head)[a]

	1968	1969	1970	1971
1. Co-operative: loan	6,821	6,816	6,992	7,776
2. Corporation: loan and grant	60,238	48,630	39,876	51,674
3. Grants as % of (2)	76	77	70	76
4. (1) as % of (2)	11	14	18	15

Source: Statistical Centre of Iran (1976: 184, 216)

Notes: a For co-operatives 'per head' stands for 'per borrower' and for corporations it stands for 'per shareholder'

Since the organized credit market did not meet the credit need of most small farmers, they were forced to borrow in the informal credit market. One decade after the reform began, about half of the total agricultural credit was still obtained on the latter market, i.e. from moneylenders, shopkeepers, relatives, etc. (see Table 7.1). In fact, these were the only sources of credit which were available to many peasants since they did not have co-operative societies. But even the peasants who had access to co-operative loans often had to obtain non-institutional credit to supplement co-operative loans. In many cases, loans which were obtained from moneylenders, shopkeepers, relatives, etc., constituted between 40 and 80 per cent of the peasants' total loans (see Momeni 1980: 406–7; Khosrovi 1979b: 160–1; Denman 1973: 201). These loans generally carried interest rates which amounted to between 20 and 50 per cent (see, among others, Momeni 1980: 407–8; Aresvik 1976: 169).[7]

In sum, the peasants' loans consisted of low, short-term institutional credits and loans financed by moneylenders at notoriously high interest rates. Such loans could hardly be used for productive investments and as a result they were principally spent on current agricultural expenditure and consumption (see Khosrovi 1979b: 157; Momeni 1980: 391–4; Hooglund 1982: 96, 110). On the other hand, as would be expected in a bimodal agrarian system, the Iranian large farmers generally had easier access to long- and medium-term institutional credits.

The rural labour market

We saw that large farmers controlled land and water in the Iranian rural areas and had also easier access to capital. Theoretically, this situation may give large landowners some power even in the village labour market since there are normally few employment opportunities near by other than the farms of large farmers. One can hardly expect small farms to provide any significant employment for outsiders. These farms often have difficulty in providing sufficient work even for family members. There are reasons to believe that large farmers could have gained some power in labour markets in the Iranian villages after the reform.

Table 7.5 shows, for example, that about 70 per cent of farms under 10 hectares were cultivated exclusively by family members and 26 per cent of such land employed few additional labourers. In fact, numerous small farmers could not rely entirely on their farms for their living and, therefore, they had to seek jobs on other farms (see Chapter 6, pp. 108–9; Hooglund 1982: 97). Moreover, some peasants lost their rights to land in one way or another in different stages of the land reform and became landless labourers. Consequently, competition for the available jobs in each village, or in close neighbouring villages, could have increased, which in turn

Table 7.5 Percentage share of wage labour in total labour employed by farms of different size-groups, 1974

Farm size (hectares)	Only family labour	Mainly family labour	Mainly wage labour
< 10	70	26	4
10−50	44	48	7
> 50	15	39	47
All farms	66	29	5

Source: Khosrovi (1981: 53)

would have increased the influence of large farmers in their local labour market.

However, the increasing non-agricultural employment opportunities operated against such a likely outcome. The oil boom of the early 1970s created an enormous demand for labour, especially for unskilled labour. Demand increases occurred mainly in the urban areas which led to a widening gap between rural and urban wages (Kazemi 1980: 42; see also Khosrovi 1979: 112−13). This, and the gloomy employment outlook in the rural areas, might have been the main reason behind the mass rural−urban migration of the 1970s. It has been estimated that about 2 million villagers, or more than 70 per cent of the population increase in villages, migrated to cities in the period 1966 to 1976 (Hooglund 1982: 118−19; see also Kazemi 1980: 14). The existence of a great outlet for surplus labour must have helped to reduce rural unemployment to the low level of about 3 per cent in 1976.[8]

Although the availability of non-agricultural employment was beneficial to the rural surplus labour, it might have been detrimental to the agricultural sector in general and poor peasants in particular. The loss of too many labourers was in fact a resource movement out of agriculture which might have affected agricultural production adversely (see pp. 132−4). The migration of the labour force was perhaps more troublesome for small farmers since an increasing number of family members left the villages and they thus lost their principal, and relatively cheap, production factor. In consequence, they had to turn to wage labour. It seems that many of them could not afford this and chose instead to cultivate less land than before (cf. Hooglund 1982: 120; see also Haririan 1976: 341−2; Saeedi 1975: 652). On the other hand large farmers, who might have faced labour shortages and increasing wages, began to employ 'imported' Afghani labourers who demanded lower wages than the prevailing ones (Hooglund 1982: 87, 116, 120; see also Mahdavi 1982: 61).

Modernization of farming techniques after the reform

Some of the landowners had begun large-scale farming before the reform. They tended to utilize new technology on their farms and especially invested in tractors. Such activities were interrupted when the land reform and anti-feudal campaign started in 1962. For example, a government agency imported agricultural machinery and sold it to agricultural companies and landowners before the reform, but since the demand for agricultural machinery decreased after the reform, the agency curtailed its activities in 1963 (Bank Markazi Iran, *Annual Report and Balance Sheet* 1965: 131; see also Momeni 1980: 323–4). However, landlords generally began to invest in modern technology after they succeeded in controlling the reform and became more involved in agricultural activities. Table 7.6, which shows the sales of tractors and combines in the years immediately before and after the reform, reflects this trend very clearly.

Table 7.6 Sales of tractors and combines, 1961–5

	1961	1962	1963	1964	1965
Tractors	1,223	645	133	714	6,300
Combines	168	195	6	36	91

Sources: Statistical Centre of Iran (1971: 44); Katouzian (1978: 365)

Table 7.6 also shows that there was a tremendous increase in the sale of tractors in 1965. This might be partly attributed to the implementation of the second stage of the land reform. The land which was worked by labourers and ploughed by mechanized means was exempted from land reform during this stage.[9] However, the modernization process continued after the reform and the application of tractors, different kinds of fertilizers and pesticides, etc., became more common in agriculture in Iran. Table 7.7 illustrates the increase in the use of three major technical inputs after the reform. We can see that the amount of fertilizers had increased by more than 4,000 times, and tractors by about eight times up to 1977.

Notwithstanding large increases in the application of modern inputs, the employment of these inputs was far from being comprehensive enough to cover all 2.5 million Iranian farmers. The available statistics show, for example, that there were wide differences in the use of machinery in various parts of the country. In some regions such as Sistan and Baluchestan, Yazd and Ilam, the amount of machinery in use was negligible in 1972 (Statistical Centre of Iran 1976: 199). At the same time, the bulk of all types of machinery was concentrated in several regions (see Table 7.8). Among these regions

Mazandaran, Khorasan and Markazi provinces had comparatively more large farms (Hooglund 1982: 83; Azkia 1986: 218; Khosrovi 1981: 91). Moreover, a large number of farm corporations were located in Fars (see Azkia 1986: 244).[10] It is then reasonable to believe that it was mainly large farmers who employed machinery on their farms (cf. Agah Book Collection 1982: 165–6; Khosrovi 1982: 47; Momeni 1980: 326–7).

Table 7.7 The application of machinery and fertilizer to agriculture, selected years

Years	No. of combines	No. of tractors	Fertilizers (tons)
1962	900	6,000	18,000
1967	n.a.	17,500	49,000
1971	1,800	23,000	32,800
1977	2,500	53,000	772,000

Sources: Statistical Centre of Iran (1976, 1984); *Iran Almanac* (1963: 263); FAO, *Production Yearbook* (1966, 1971)

Table 7.8 Distribution of machinery by selected provinces, 1972 (percentage)

Province	Tractors	Combines	Other machinery
Fars	6	8	5
Khorasan	13	2	10
Kordestan	7	11	<1[a]
Markazi	10	5	2
Mazandaran	18	53	50
West Azarbayjan	10	5	<1
Rest of the country	36	16	33

Source: Statistical Centre of Iran (1976: 199)

Note: a Less than 1 per cent

The application of modern technology was comparatively widespread in Mazandaran. According to Table 7.8, Mazandaran was the most mechanized region of the country in 1972. Large-scale, modern farming had begun in this region, which mostly belonged to the royal family, before the land reform (see Chapter 3, pp. 32–3, 40). In spite of the land reform and the redistribution of crown lands, large farms prevailed in this region after the reform. Moreover, many of these farms belonged to influential figures such as members of the royal family, high-rank army officers, lawyers, etc. (see Nikayin 1976: 78–9; Momeni 1980: 300–1). One of the shah's brothers had a farm in this region which was as large as

3,000 hectares and was cultivated with twenty tractors, nine combines, thirteen tillers, etc. (Mohammadi 1973: 39–40).

Large farmers were generally inclined to use labour-saving methods. As a result, mechanization of major operations such as ploughing and harvesting became very common on large farms (see Momeni 1980: 325–6; Aresvik 1976: 164; Hooglund 1982: 97; Antoun 1976: 8). Unfortunately, we have little information about individual large farms but there is more information about agri-businesses and farm corporations which shows that they followed a labour-saving, capital-intensive policy. It was because of this policy that the use of tractors and combines in farm corporations increased to 100 per cent and 95 per cent, respectively, of the culti-vated area in 1975 (Ashraf and Banuazizi 1980: 41). Sometimes the houses in the villages covered by corporations were bulldozed to make sure that the surplus labour would go elsewhere. New accom-modation was subsequently built only for the retained workers and their families (Platt 1970: 81). However, if the labourers had not been driven out of the villages by force, the decreasing employment opportunities on corporations would have forced them to migrate (Azkia 1980: 221, 239; see also Aresvik 1976: 123).

From the outset, the emphasis of agribusinesses was on capital-intensive methods. The agribusinesses which were established below the Dez Dam in Khuzestan provide a good example. Here only 6,000 labourers were employed on 68,000 hectares, i.e. one worker for every 11 hectares of irrigated land; peasant holdings employed one person for every 2 hectares (Dumont 1978: 17). The tendency to use capital-intensive methods on larger farms was accompanied by relatively extensive use of land. We can see from Table 7.9 that the amount of land which was left fallow increased as farms became larger. It should be borne in mind that land, first and foremost, was left fallow because of water shortage. However, the land of large farmers was generally very fertile with easier access to water and it could have been cultivated more intensively than the small farms. The extensive land use and the increasing tendency of large farmers to employ capital-intensive methods lend support in part to our earlier conclusion that land and capital would be cheaper for large farmers than the peasants in a bimodal system (see Chapter 4, pp. 54–9).

In addition to its credit policy, the government supported the development of capital-intensive methods in different ways. For example, all the machinery which agribusinesses needed to import for their activities was exempted from import taxes, provided that such machinery was not produced in the country (Azkia 1980: 126–7). A government agency was also responsible for importing tractors and selling them to farmers on instalment.

Table 7.9 Distribution of fallow land by farm size, 1974 (hectares)

Farm size	Total area	Fallow land	Fallow land as % of total area
< 10	5,389,877	1,589,154	29
10–30	6,391,526	2,413,456	38
> 30	4,635,818	1,952,737	42
All farms	16,417,221	5,955,347	36

Source: Khosrovi (1981: 57; 1982: 68)

Some attempts were made by the government to introduce improved seeds in agriculture but they had little effect. Accordingly, high-yielding varieties of wheat and improved cottonseed, vegetable seeds, fruit shoots, etc., were distributed among farmers. Considering the fact that wheat had been the staple crop in Iran, the spread of high-yielding varieties of wheat would have largely benefited small farmers. However, the programme which aimed at extending the use of high-yielding varieties of wheat suffered from serious shortcomings, and as late as 1976 the improved varieties were cultivated on only about 350,000 hectares of irrigated land. Inadequate supply of improved seeds and fertilizers, and insufficient work, etc., were responsible for the limited effects of the programme (Aresvik 1976: 136–43).

It is necessary to point out that the modernization process was not strictly confined to large farms. There were also many farmers with medium-sized holdings and some prosperous small farmers who began to use new methods of production. For example, the upper strata of small farmers in Gilan and Mazandaran, who were considerably better off than most of their counterparts in the rest of the country, increasingly used two-wheel tractors on their farms (Khosrovi 1981: 144–5; Aresvik 1976: 160–3). Moreover, a recent statistical study shows that small farmers in fact used more fertilizers per hectare on all their land than the large farmers in 1974 (Agah Book Collection 1982: 185). The data for the consumption of fertilizers in 1971 shows, however, that around 74 per cent of all fertilizers were only used in five provinces (Statistical Centre of Iran 1976: 185).[11] Among these Esfahan, Gilan and Mazandaran are known to have comparatively prosperous peasants which suggests that it might again have been the richer peasants who mostly used fertilizers.

On the whole, there is some evidence which suggests that the large farmers generally tended to modernize their farming after the land reform. There were also small peasants who, sometimes jointly, invested in agricultural machinery, began to use fertilizers, improved seeds, etc., and who hired tractors for ploughing (see, for example, Momeni 1980: 322–7; Craig 1978: 148; Lambton 1969: 224–8). However, the great majority of peasants experienced little change in their farming techniques and relied predominantly on the traditional methods of production in the late 1970s.

The new agrarian system and agricultural production

We saw in Chapter 3 that most of the cropland was under food-grains, i.e. wheat, barley and rice, before the reform. Cash crops such as cotton, sugar beets, fruits, and oil seeds occupied only a small proportion of all the cultivated land.[12] Parallel to other changes in the agrarian system after the land reform, this crop pattern also began to change. Accordingly, more and more land was allocated to cash crops and the comparative share of land under staple food products declined. Table 7.10 summarizes this trend.

The table shows that although the land under cultivation increased for both staple food crops and cash crops, during the period 1960 to 1975, the latter increased much more markedly than

Table 7.10 Land under staple and cash crops, 1960–75 (thousand hectares)

Type of crop	1960		1975		% change
Foodgrains[a]		5,579		7,778	39
Irrigated	(2,080)		(2,318)		(11)
Unirrigated	(3,499)		(5,463)		(56)
Cash crops[b]		1,126		2,670	131
Irrigated	(619)		(1,786)[c]		(189)
Unirrigated	(507)		(884)		(74)
Others		98		168	71
Irrigated	(78)		(137)[c]		(76)
Unirrigated	(20)		(31)		(55)
Total		6,803		10,616	56
Foodgrains as % of total		82		73	– 11

Source: Agah Book Collection (1982: 181)

Notes: a Mainly wheat, barley, and rice
b Cotton, sugar beets, vegetables, fruits, etc.
c The distinction between irrigated and non-irrigated land for fruit and non-fruit for 1975 was not available; consequently 1976 data were used

the former. Consequently, the share of food grain land decreased from 82 per cent of the cultivated land to 73 per cent in 1975 (see Table 7.10). Its share dropped further to about 70 per cent in 1978 (Statistical Centre of Iran 1984: 335). Table 7.10 also shows that the share of cash crops was partly increased at the expense of staple crops (cf. Agah Book Collection 1982: 163). Moreover, it clearly illustrates that cash crop cultivation was developed predominantly on irrigated land while the increase in foodgrain land mainly consisted of unirrigated, and probably less fertile land (see also Aresvik 1976: 49).

As was pointed out in Chapter 1, there are frequent discrepancies between the crop production data which are given out by different official sources (see p. 3). As a result, different sources may give different pictures of the changes in crop production after the reform. This is clearly reflected in Table 7.11 which illustrates production data for the staple and cash crops by the two major sources of agricultural statistics, namely the Statistical Centre of Iran and the Ministry of Agriculture.

The two sources indicate a similar trend in crop production up to 1973. They show that although the production of all crops increased, cash crop production, as a whole, grew more rapidly (see Table 7.11). On the other hand, they produce a rather different picture for the period after 1973. The data of the Statistical Centre show that the same trend persisted even after 1973 while the very high figures of the Ministry of Agriculture for staple crops obscure this trend in its statistics. The fact that imports of foodgrains increased from 904,000 tons in 1973 to about 1,804,000 tons in 1974 and remained high in the following years seems to suggest that (i) the production of staple food products could not have been as favourable as the Ministry of Agriculture reported, and (ii) the data of the Statistical Centre of Iran, as was mentioned earlier, are comparatively more reliable (see Bank Markazi Iran, *Annual Report and Balance Sheet* 1976: 79).

Table 7.12, which is based on the data provided by the Ministry of Agriculture, provides a detailed illustration of the growth of agricultural products for a period when the production statistics of the two sources are largely in agreement with each other. We can see from Table 7.12 that all agricultural products increased in this period but cash crops increased more steadily. The growth rates of wheat and barley, which were comparatively high between 1963 and 1967, fell close to zero in the following period. On the other hand, most cash crops increased at higher rates in the second period.

There are several reasons to believe that large farmers might have

Table 7.11 Production of staple and cash crops by source of information, 1968–77 (thousand tons)

Source of information and year	Staple crops[a]	Cash crops[b]
A. Statistical Centre		
1968	5,995	4,538
1971	5,340	4,988
1972	6,633	5,136
1973	6,641	6,003
1974	4,463	5,766
1975	6,408	6,298
1977	5,779	5,416[c]
B. Ministry of Agriculture		
1968	5,990	4,576[d]
1971	5,650	5,304
1972	6,755	5,400
1973	6,857	6,177
1974	6,876	6,418
1975	8,330	6,580
1977	8,130	5,961[e]

Sources: Agah Book Collection (1982: 182–3); Bank Markazi Iran, *Annual Report and Balance Sheet* (1972–7)

Notes: a Wheat, barley and rice
b Cotton, sugar beet, tobacco, pulses, sugar cane and oil seeds
c For pulses the data of the Ministry of Agriculture were used
d For tobacco the data of the Statistical Centre were used
e For sugar cane the data of the Statistical Centre were used

been mainly responsible for the increase in the land under cash crops and in cash production. First, the process of bimodal-oriented changes which started in 1963 must have progressed greatly by 1968. This process was very likely reinforced by the landlord-biased agricultural policies and the third stage of land reform. They were mainly initiated in 1968 (see Chapter 5, pp. 83–5). Consequently, large farmers were certainly more active in farming after 1968 and the coincidence of the increase of growth rates of cash crops with this increased activity may indicate that there was probably a positive relationship between the two trends.

Second, since orchards were exempted from the land reform, many landlords extended their former orchards or planted new ones to retain their land (see Chapter 6, p. 94). Moreover, fruits and nuts were much more profitable than staple crops and this must also have encouraged farmers to develop orchards.[13] However, it would take time before orchards came to bear fruit and most peasants could not afford it. Thus it was in all probability large owners and more prosperous farmers who planted most of the fruit-bearing trees after the land reform. As a result, the orchard

127

land increased by about 60 per cent and the number of trees by 50 per cent between 1960 and 1972 (Statistical Centre of Iran: 1976: 193, 207).

Table 7.12 Annual growth rates of crop production, selected periods (percentage)

	1963–7	1968–72
Grains		
Wheat	7.1	0.5
Barley	6.2	−0.7
Rice	6.5	4.6
Pulses	9	4.7
Vegetables		
Potatoes	3.1	−1
Onions	3.9	7.7
Tomatoes	3.8	3.1[a]
Melons	3.6	5.9
Industrial crops		
Cotton	4.5	7.8
Sugar beet	27	7.7
Oil seed	8.5	24.8
Fruit[a]		
Citrus	4.4	6.2
Apples	4	21.1
Grapes	0.2	6.8

Source: Aresvik (1976: 251)

Note: a 1972 data were not available and thus the growth rates for the second period refer to 1968–71

Third, cash crops needed comparatively more water and were therefore mainly cultivated on irrigated land (see Table 7.1). We saw earlier that peasants generally had difficult access to water and they could have contributed only marginally to the increase of cash crops. Finally, farmers often had to learn the cultivation of 'new' crops. Moreover, cultivation of cash crops requires more cash and involves difficulties such as buying new inputs and selling the crop. We have already seen that a large majority of peasants had considerable difficulty in rasing loans or obtaining new inputs such as fertilizers and consequently were not able to cultivate cash crops easily. There were even cases where the peasants reduced their cash crop cultivation or stopped it altogether after the reform since they lost their landlords' financial support (see Momeni 1980: 332).

The available data also reveal that cash crop production was in general concentrated in certain regions. Table 7.13 shows, for example, that production of several major cash crops, including rice, was highly concentrated in only four regions. The comparatively higher proportion of large farms in Mazandaran and Khorasan and the existence of the largest number of farm corporations in Fars could have contributed to such a concentration (see Azkia 1986: 244).[14] On the other hand, a large majority of rice-growers, who were predominantly small farmers, were Gilani and Mazandarani peasants (see Kamali 1982). They were normally more prosperous than their counterparts in the rest of the country. Perhaps most of the small cotton cultivators were also Mazandarani peasants. They were encouraged to shift to cotton by the success of large farmers who had initiated its cultivation (see Okazaki 1968: 28–35). Large farmers in fact diffused the know-how of cotton cultivation in the region and demonstrated its profitability which together reduced the risk of shifting to the 'new' crop for the peasants. Finally, we can see from Table 7.13 that the concentration of production of cotton, sugar beet and rice in the above-mentioned provinces increased further between 1973 and 1978.

All in all, it is plausible to conclude that it was especially the large and more prosperous farmers who were in a position to produce cash crops. In fact, they increasingly did so. Many studies emphasize that those farmers allocated more and more land and capital to cash crops such as cotton, sugar beet and oil seeds (see Momeni 1980: 333; Hooglund 1982: 112; Haririan 1976: 340).

Table 7.13 Production shares of selected provinces in the total production of principal cash crops, 1973 and 1978

Province	1973			1978		
	Cotton	Sugar beets	Rice	Cotton	Sugar beets	Rice
Fars	10	12	4	4	20	10
Gilan	—	—	44	—	—	50
Khorasan	11	45	—	13	46	—
Mazandaran	65	—	41	76	—	34
Total	86	57	89	93	66	94

Source: Statistical Centre of Iran (1984: 281–4)

Staple food crops and agricultural growth

In spite of the gradual shift from staple crops to cash crops, the former continued to be predominant in Iran. Wheat, barley and rice comprised 51, 15, and 3 per cent, respectively, of cultivated land as late as 1978 (Statistical Centre of Iran 1984: 335). Most of this land, except rice land, was rain-fed and more than 80 per cent of it belonged to peasants. In consequence, changes in the production and productivity of staple food products had decisive effects on both agricultural growth and peasant living standards.

Scarcity of credit and lack of peasant-biased innovations, which are typical in a bimodal agrarian system, hindered peasants from improving the production of staple crops. Large farms also failed to invest in these crops. The main investment of many large farmers in staple crops seems to have involved the mechanization of wheat and barley production and the expansion of their production in unirrigated land (see Aresvik 1976: 53). Consequently, rates of land productivity for wheat and barley were stagnant and remained low after the land reform. The yield per hectare for rice improved to some degree during this period (cf. Kamali 1982: 142–3; Katouzian 1983: 327–8). On the other hand, the yield of cash crops, e.g. sugar beet and cotton, increased rather well in the post-reform period (cf. Aresvik 1976: 49–50). Table 7.14 summarizes the changes in yields of five major crops after the reform. We have to note that the FAO figures for staple crops are usually higher than those of the Statistical Centre of Iran, especially in more recent years. For example, according to the data of the Statistical Centre of Iran, the yields (kilograms per hectare) of the above crops in 1977–8 were as follows: wheat 807, barley 791, rice 2,457, sugar beet 26,442 and cotton 1,778 (Statistical Centre of Iran 1984: 278, 284, 335).

Table 7.14 Yield of major crops in Iran, 1961–78 (kilograms per hectare)

Crop	1961–5	1966–70	1971–5	1977–8	Average of near east region 1977–8	Average of developing countries 1977–8
Wheat	802	896	884	1,011	1,408	1,347
Barley	800	891	753	841	1,204	1,218
Rice	2,914	3,355	3,455	3,315	3,866	2,484
Cotton	939	1,198	1,650	1,598	1,762	914
Sugar beets	19,202	21,082	24,243	25,314	31,088	30,938

Source: FAO, *Production Yearbook* (1971–9)

The government's price policy was an important factor which discouraged farmers from investing in staple crops and improving their production. This was a particular deterrent in the case of wheat which was by far the most important crop. The price policy for wheat, which started in the early 1960s, aimed to stabilize the wholesale price of wheat in order to prevent, above all, increases in the price of bread in the cities and at the same time guarantee a minimum price to the producers. However, this policy suffered from certain shortcomings and failed to benefit wheat producers. (The following three paragraphs are largely based on Aresvik 1976: 143–9).

First, the minimum price of wheat which was set by the government was rather low in comparison to its production costs. Between 1960 and 1974, the minimum prices of wheat remained almost unchanged while all other prices increased. In 1974, the minimum price was raised by 40 per cent but this price and the following revisions in the minimum price were not realistic either. In 1978, for example, the floor price of wheat was 12 rials per kilo but the production costs to the farmer averaged between 14 and 17 rials per kilo (Hooglund 1982: 114).

Second, the minimum price used to be announced every year after the wheat harvest was partly over. This made it ineffective as a floor price for the producers and could naturally not affect their decision to improve wheat production. In fact, by such a late date, most farmers, especially the small farmers, had already entered into contracts with private wholesalers at prices which were usually lower than the minimum price subsequently announced (Hooglund 1982: 113). In good crop years, wheat was often sold at up to 40 per cent less than the official prices.

Third, the Cereals Organization, which was responsible for carrying out the government's wheat policy, was not ready to buy all the wheat offered at the official minimum price. The purchases of this organization comprised only a small proportion of total wheat production and never reached even 6 per cent of total production by 1974.[15] Consequently, even after a considerable increase in the official floor price in 1974 and the government's decision to expand its purchase, most of the peasants did not regard sales to the Cereals Organization as a realistic alternative (see Aresvik 1976: 145; Hooglund 1982: 113). As late as 1975, only about 8 per cent of total wheat production was sold to the Cereals Organization. Pre-harvest buyers, dealers, shopkeepers, etc., continued to be the major, and often the only, alternatives which were available for peasants wishing to sell their products.

On the whole, this policy did not benefit wheat growers and failed to stimulate them to invest in yield-improving practices. It also did not succeed in pegging the wholesale prices of wheat which fluctuated widely during this period (Aresvik 1976: 145–6). In order to control the price of bread in the urban areas and fill the gap between the growing demand and sluggish supply of wheat, the government increasingly imported wheat. The amount of imported wheat increased from 127,000 tons in 1962 to 1,440,000 tons in

1975 (Bank Markazi Iran, *Annual Report and Balance Sheet* 1966, 1976; the figure for 1962 includes both wheat and flour imports). It is worth noting that the total cost of each ton of imported wheat exceeded the price of each ton of wheat which the government was ready to pay to the Iranian farmers. For example, the imported wheat cost the government 13,400 rials per ton in 1975 while it paid only 10,000 rials for domestic wheat (Azkia 1986: 165–6; see also Aresvik 1976: 149). The government subsequently sold the wheat to millers at 10,000 rials per ton. In other words, the imported wheat was subsidized by 3,400 rials per ton (see Azkia 1986: 165–6; Aresvik 1976: 149).

Broadly speaking, the stagnation of staple food production adversely affected the agricultural growth rates in the post-reform years. According to the official figures, agriculture grew at the annual rate of 4.5 per cent during the period 1962–7, 2.6 per cent during the period 1967–72, and 4.9 per cent during the period 1972–7 (Katouzian 1983: 320–1). Considering the population growth rate of 3 per cent per annum, per capita agricultural production might have increased slowly after the reform. This is clearly reflected in the FAO statistics which are illustrated in Table 7.15. Such growth rates, however, overestimate the real growth rates. These figures are in all probability based on the statistics of the Ministry of Agriculture. Many researchers estimate that the real agricultural growth rates might have been 2 to 3 per cent per annum after the reform (see among others, Katouzian 1983: 320–1; Dumont 1978: 8–9; Halliday 1979: 126–7).

Table 7.15 Production indices of agriculture, 1967–77 (1969–71 = 100)

Year	Total agriculture	Per capita agriculture
1967	87	95
1969	99	102
1971	100	97
1973	117	107
1975	128	110
1977	132	107

Source: FAO, *Production Yearbook* (1979: 78, 82)

In sum, the growth of most of the agricultural products, especially staple crops, failed to meet domestic needs. The government then imported an increasing amount of agricultural products in order to satisfy domestic demand, particularly after sharp increases of oil revenues in 1973. As a result, the gap between the value of exports and imports of agricultural products widened rapidly after the reform and the gain to the country from exporting some cash crops fell far below its costs of importing food products (see Table 7.16).

Table 7.16 Value of agricultural exports and imports, 1961–73 (million rials)

	1961–3	1966–8	1971–3
Exports	6,167	8,521	15,762
Imports	6,353	9,140	25,069
Balance	−186	−619	−9,307

Source: Aresvik (1976: 224)

We must point out that our theoretical analysis concluded that there could be rapid agricultural growth even in a bimodal agrarian system (see Chapter 4, pp. 59–61). This implies that the sluggish agricultural growth in Iran can hardly be explained by the post-reform agrarian system alone. There must be some other factors behind the unsatisfactory performance of the agricultural sector as well. The oil-boom of the early 1970s was perhaps the most important contributing factor.

The 'Dutch disease' theory provides a theoretical ground to believe that the boom in one sector of an economy, such as the oil industry, might cause a decline in another sectors, e.g. agriculture. In its simplest version, the theory argues that a booming sector would influence a non-booming sector through a resource move-ment effect and a spending effect (see, among others, Corden and Neary 1982; Benjamin *et al.* 1989; Scherr 1989). The former draws resources out of the non-booming sector while the latter turns rela-tive prices against it. We saw earlier that a mass rural–urban migration followed the 1970s' oil-boom in Iran which presumably caused serious problems for the peasantry. This resource move-ment out of agriculture must have had some negative impact on the performance of the sector.[16]

We maintain, however, that the 'Dutch disease' may damage an agricultural sector more seriously in a bimodal agrarian system than in a unimodal system. The intersectoral mobility of produc-tion factors is likely to be greater in a bimodal system and this makes the agricultural sector more vulnerable to the pressures of a booming sector. To put it more precisely, landless labourers and small peasants who can hardly make a living in agriculture would very easily respond to the employment opportunities elsewhere. On the contrary, peasants with viable farms would likely need a much stronger incentive to leave their villages. Moreover, it is relatively easy for large landowners, who have very often had other non-agricultural activities, to move their capital to more beneficial sectors. Small farmers have usually little capital and lack the experience to do so.

Concluding remarks

Generally speaking, the differences between large and small Iranian farmers were more noticeable in relation to the size of their land and their access to irrigation water in the initial period of the post-reform era. But, as expected in a bimodal agrarian system, the differences tended to spread to every aspect of their economic lives. To begin with the large farmers could more easily receive large, long-term credits especially from the government institutions, sometimes at very low rates of interest. On the other hand, the peasants had access generally to small, short-term loans which were extended to them through the rural co-operative societies. Not infrequently, they could not even receive such loans or the loans fell short of their immediate needs. Consequently, they had to borrow money from moneylenders at very high interest rates.

There were also growing differences between the production methods used by the two groups. The large farmers were generally inclined to modernize their farming, mainly through capital-intensive methods, while the majority of the peasants continued to rely on traditional methods of production, which meant they continued to depend on the normally abundant peasant labour force. However, the oil-boom and the following mass rural—urban migration deprived many peasants of their relatively cheap labour. In some cases, this led to a reduction of the cultivated area of peasants' farms.

Finally, large farmers tended increasingly to substitute cultivation of more profitable cash crops for that of the staple crops. it was also the increase in cash-crop production that was responsible for much of the agricultural growth, which at most seems to have matched population growth after the reform. This implies that the production of staple food crops lagged behind the rapidly increasing food demand which resulted from population growth and income rises. The country was then forced to import an increasing amount of food products each year. In general, the government's agricultural policies and the oil boom tended to reinforce the above process.

Chapter eight

Rural poverty and inequality after the reform

The previous chapter showed that the development of a bimodal agrarian system after the land reform in Iran was accompanied by certain imperfections in the rural factor markets and resulted in growing differences between large and small farmers with respect to their farming methods and the kinds of crops that they grew. In addition to land, large farmers enjoyed easier access to water, employed modern, capital-intensive techniques, and increasingly cultivated cash crops. On the other hand, most of the peasants continued to use the traditional methods of cultivation and predominantly grew wheat and barley.

We did not, however, discuss the effects of the changes that followed the land reform on rural poverty and inequality. According to the theoretical analysis in Chapter 4, if a land reform leads to a bimodal agrarian system, it can hardly improve the lot of the majority of the rural people and reduce rural inequalities. The aim of our concluding chapter is to see if this was true in the Iranian rural areas after the reform. In other words, we want to find out whether the rural poor in Iran experienced any meaningful improvement in their living conditions after the reform.

Prevalence of subsistence farming

We saw earlier that the post-reform conditions in the Iranian rural economy generally preclude the majority of peasants from investing in land and improving their traditional methods of cultivation. As a result, many peasants could hardly have experienced substantial increases in their production after the reform. Considering the fact that the peasants predominantly produce food crops and usually sold only their surpluses, Table 8.1 suggests that a large proportion of the peasants lack any surplus over and above their own consumption. This is especially true for small farmers because that part of their crops which they sold was not always in excess of their own consumption: they sold it because they needed to buy other necessities such as sugar and tea (Khosrovi 1981: 27). However, we can see from Table 8.1 that there were substantial regional variations. In more prosperous regions, e.g. Gilan, peasants were more market-oriented particularly because of favourable natural conditions and/or better access to the urban market. On the contrary, almost all peasants were subsistence farmers in less fertile regions such as Sistan and Baluchestan where a negligible percentage of farmers produced mainly for the market.

Table 8.1 Distribution of farmers by share of crop sold and by farm size, 1974 (percentage)

Farm size	Not sold	Partially sold[a]	Mainly sold[b]
< 10	53	27	21
10–50	48	28	23
< 50	2	1	97
All holdings:			
1. Iran	51	27	22
2. Gilan	26	25	49
3. Markazi	34	34	32
4. Sistan and Baluchestan	86	10	4

Source: Khosrovi (1981)

Notes: a Less than 50 per cent of the produce was sold
        b At least 50 per cent was sold

As we can see, the information provided by Table 8.1 concerns only the annual crops, especially wheat and barley. Nevertheless, considering other agricultural products, such as fruits and poultry, does not change the general picture. According to the available data, a comparatively larger proportion of orchard products was sold by the peasants while the share of their sale of livestock production was lower than those of the annual crops (Khosrovi 1981: 21, 52). A higher rate of commercialization of permanent crops, especially among small farmers, might reflect the fact that some small farms consisted entirely of orchards and were market-oriented in nature. If we could exclude the marketed products of this group of farmers, we would very likely find out that the rest of the orchard products were principally consumed by the peasants themselves. On the whole, it is plausible to conclude that self-consumption was still the prime motive of most peasants in post-reform agriculture (cf. Khosrovi 1979: 98–102; Hooglund 1982: 93–4).

We should note, however, that self-consumption does not necessarily mean self-sufficiency. A rough estimate, for example, indicates that peasants with less than 2 hectares (i.e. 43 per cent of the Iranian farmers) produced only 28 per cent of their total wheat consumption in 1978 (Khosrovi 1982: 30). Despite the short-comings of such estimates, it is reasonable to believe that the production of many peasants, especially the smaller ones, was less than their consumption.[1]

One reason for the lack of improvement in the production of most small peasants and the persistence of the subsistence economy in most of the Iranian villages must have been the small size of the peasants' farms (see Hooglund 1982: 93–4). In fact, given the pre-vailing farming practices, more than 70 per cent of the farmers received farms which were smaller than the size which is generally considered to be essential for a subsistence standard of living, i.e. 7 hectares (see Chapter 6, pp. 108–9). This was, however, a less important factor compared with the post-reform agrarian system. If the peasants had not been deprived of improving their produc-tion methods by the bimodal mechanism, they might have largely overcome the size problem and increased their production. This fact is clearly reflected in a study carried out by the World Bank in 1975 (see Price 1975, cited in Aresvik 1976: 102–4).

Table 8.2 Approximate size of farms required from $500 income per capita (hectares)

Type of farm	Common practices in 1975	Improved practices
Dryland cereal farm	70	40
Partly irrigated field-crop farm[a]	9	5
Intensively irrigated field-crop farm[b]	5	3.3
Rice farm	2.5	1.5
Orchard	0.6	0.35

Source: Aresvik (1976: 104)

Notes: a 60% wheat, 30% sugar beets or similar crops and 10% fallow
b 90% sugar beets, vegetables, and similar crops, and 10% fallow

According to the above study, a peasant family would attain an income of $500 per member in 1980 from a considerably smaller farm if the peasant was able to modernize his farm. For example, we can see from Table 8.2 that applying improved practices would almost halve the size a partially irrigated field-crop farm required to meet the target income. Table 8.2 also reveals that the income of a great number of small farmers must have been considerably lower than the target income in 1975: their farms were comparatively too small with respect to the fact that they suffered from insufficient access to water, applied the traditional methods and grew mainly wheat and barley. This issue, however, will be discussed in more detail in the next section.

Persistence of low levels of living in rural areas

The lack of sufficient data limits our study of the developments of the rural levels of living after the reform. The available information, however, tends to suggest that rural poverty persisted in the Iranian rural areas and the gap between rich and poor villagers might have widened.

For example, Table 8.3 which is based on a World Bank study, shows that one decade after the reform the average income of a large majority of the rural population was very low. The income of about half of the rural people even fell short of the per capita consumption in rural areas in the same year, which was about $102 (see Parvin and Zamani 1979: 47; we assumed that 73 rials = $1). This means that these people, who were principally landless labourers and the very small farmers, could not even afford the average rural consumption, which was lower than the nation-wide consumption level (see Table 8.4).

Table 8.3 Per capita rural income, 1972 (US dollars)

Size of farm (hectares)	Mean income	% of rural population
<3 [a]	70	47
3–10	131	33
11–50 [b]	302	19
>50	1,000	1

Source: Halliday (1979: 132)

Notes: a Includes landless labourers
          b Includes animal herders

Table 8.4 which shows per capita consumption expenditures can be used to throw some light on changes in levels of living in rural areas. Accordingly, rural consumption increased very slowly between 1962 and 1972 and rose sharply after the oil-boom in 1973. Considering the fact that official statistics were notoriously inclined to report good results, even Table 8.4 suggests that there had been little change in rural standards of living up to 1973. All in all, the official figures show that rural consumption increased by about 40 per cent between 1962 and 1975. There are some facts, however, which indicate that a large number of rural families might have hardly enjoyed any improvement in their levels of consumption.

Table 8.4 Per capita consumption expenditures of the urban and rural households, selected years (1959 prices)

Year	Rural	Urban	Rural as % of urban
1959	7,012	14,923	47
1962	7,638	16,502	46
1965	8,375	16,277	51
1968	8,590	22,027	39
1971	8,036	25,866	31
1973	8,351	31,843	26
1976	10,706	40,789	26

Source: Parvin and Zamani (1974: 47)

First, Iran is characterized by numerous regional variations and, therefore, the peasants of a region, or even a village, might have considerably improved their income and consumption while some other peasants in their neighbourhood might have experienced the opposite. For example, a comparison between incomes of different regions in 1977 reveals that the peasants in West Azarbayjan earned, on average, more than 2.4 times the average income of the peasants in Kohkilouyeh and Bouyer Ahmadi (Statistical Centre of Iran 1981: 156). Similarly, monthly expenditures of a rural household in different regions varied between 11,652 and 25,392 rials in the same year (Statistical Centre of Iran 1981: 128–35; see also Asayesh 1974: 116).

Second, as Figure 8.1 demonstrates, consumption inequality increased after the reform. Thus, some peasants must have experienced a larger consumption increase than others. In fact, it has been estimated that the consumption level of the bottom 40 per cent of the rural population deteriorated between 1963 and 1973: the monthly consumption expenditures of these people declined from 2,500 rials to about 2,400 rials or less in this period (Parvin and Zamani 1979: 49).[2]

We should point out that income inequalities in the rural areas might have been more pronounced than consumption inequalities because the rich often have some savings while the poor might frequently face income deficits and thus dissave (cf. Parvin and Zamani 1979: 47–8; Katouzian 1983: 344). We may then conclude that alongside the consumption inequalities, the distribution of income also became more skewed. This is of course not unexpected in a bimodal agrarian system.

The mass rural–urban migration must have alleviated rural poverty to some extent and improved the lot of those who migrated. Nevertheless, this movement could not have led to any significant

Agriculture, poverty and reform in Iran

Figure 8.1 Lorenz curve for the rural consumption of expenditure

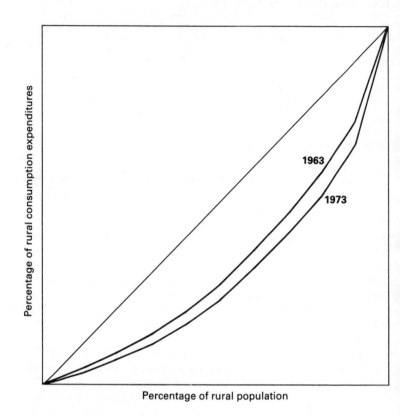

Source: Parvin and Zamani (1979: 48)

improvement in the situation of the landless labourers who remained in the villages. The small farmers could hardly afford to employ wage labour and the large farmers increasingly mechanized their farms. The availability of cheap Afghani workers did not make things easier for the rural labourers. We should remember that migration might have affected many peasants negatively since it drained them not only of surplus family labour but also of essential workers.

Irrespective of small differences, however, the rural poor generally consisted of both landless labourers and small peasants. Considering our earlier conclusion that the production of a large number of small farmers was insufficient for their own

140

consumption, one may believe that the income of many of the rural poor was not enough to reach a subsistence level. As a matter of fact, the statistics for rural incomes, which are only available for the recent years, reveal that total rural incomes fell below total rural consumption expenditure. For instance, total rural incomes in 1976, 1977 and 1978 covered only 79, 80 and 82 per cent, respectively, of total consumption expenditure (Statistical Centre of Iran 1984: 753–4). The small farmers and landless labourers must have been principally responsible for the deficits.

In many cases, field studies substantiate the above conclusions. They report that there was often a wide income gap between the villagers and that a large number of them suffered from income deficits (many examples can be found in Momeni 1980: 383–94; see further Rafipoor 1985: 206–7; Antoun 1976: 4; Mahdavi 1982: 62). In extreme cases, as many as 90 per cent of the villagers claimed that their income did not meet their living expenses (see Momeni 1980: 389–90). This may partly explain why most of the loans which were received by the peasants were spent on consumption purposes (see Chapter 7, pp. 113–19). Moreover, population growth, higher rises in the prices of the goods bought by the peasants than in the prices of their products, repayment of former debts, and lack of any significant improvement in their production might have contributed to increase income deficits and indebtedness in the rural areas.[3]

It seems that the conditions of most of the shareholders of farm corporations were not much better. These corporations, as we saw earlier, enjoyed generous government support and there are studies which show that the average income of their shareholders grew considerably after the formation of the corporations (see, for example, Denman 1978: 288–92; Azkia 1986: 246–7; Stickley and Najafi 1971: 19). But most of these studies also point out that the number of shares which each shareholder held varied greatly. Sometimes the difference between the number of shares of different shareholders of a farm corporation was about 200 shares (Khosrovi 1979b: 177; see further Momeni 1980: 368–70; Azkia 1986: 236; Mohammadi 1973: 36–7; Stickley and Najafi 1971: 19). Thus, there were plenty of shareholders whose incomes, which mainly consisted of their dividends, were hardly sufficient for life at subsistence level. They had to seek additional incomes to support themselves and thus often migrated to cities (Momeni 1980: 369–70; Azkia 1986: 242–51). This was probably one of the principal reasons that contributed to the dissolution of 88 out of the total 93 corporations and their subdivision among their shareholders, i.e. mainly the former peasants, after the 1979 Iranian Revolution.[4]

There is no question that some rural people improved their welfare after the reform. Many new, modern houses were built in rural areas, the number of the villagers who owned sewing-machines, bicycles, refrigerators, radios, etc. was on the increase, and so on. But these improvements were limited and failed to bring about any remarkable change in the living conditions of the majority of the rural people. Furthermore, these changes tended to exacerbate rural inequality.

The official statistics show that as late as 1977, about 58 per cent of the villagers had radios, 10 per cent had bicycles, 7 per cent had refrigerators, and only 3 per cent had television sets (Statistical Centre of Iran 1981: 120). It is evident that, with the exception of radios, only a minority of the rural people could have possessed such living facilities. This is clearly reflected in a sample study of the villages of a relatively less prosperous region (Yazd): 30 per cent of the sample peasants had no valuable belongings, including agricultural implements, and the total value of all belongings of another 33 per cent was less than 10,000 rials ($141) per household in 1980 (Rafipoor 1985: 216).

Table 8.5 provides further insights into the rural poverty. It illustrates, in general, that more than one decade after the reform a large proportion of rural families still lived in one or two rooms without electricity or piped water. Table 8.5 also indicates that there were large differences in housing conditions between the rural and urban areas. The fact that the majority of villagers who migrated to the cities lived in shanty towns may lead one to presume that most of the ill-conditioned houses in urban areas belonged to the rural migrants as well (see Kazemi 1980: 46–53).

Last but not least, the household expenditure surveys for rural areas in the period 1976 to 1978 reveal that around 50 per cent of

Table 8.5   Housing in rural and urban areas, 1976

Description of houses	Rural areas		Urban areas	
	No. (thousands)	%	No. (thousands)	%
Made of traditional materials[a]	2,381	81	676	28
Without electricity	2,512	86	234	10
Without piped water	2,297	78	255	11
With one room	568	19	167	7
With two rooms	1,029	35	557	23

Source: Statistical Centre of Iran (1984)

Note: a This includes all houses which are made of sun-dried brick and wooden beam, sun-dried brick and mud, wood, straw, etc. as well as tents the consumption expenditure was devoted to foodstuffs. This percentage was probably higher for the poorer villages. Nevertheless, there is reason to believe that many of them were undernourished. A study from 1972 shows that between 30 to 40 per cent of the rural population suffered from malnutrition: 700,000 of these people, or 4 per cent of the villagers, were severely undernourished in the sense that they received 75 per cent or less of a certain minimum calorie requirement (Katouzian 1983: 346–8).[5]

Conclusion

The Iranian agrarian system in the early 1960s displayed the major features of traditional tenancy systems that have often been criticized for the prevalence of agricultural backwardness and rural poverty in many developing countries. Sharecropping was the predominant form of tenure in the Iranian peasant–landlord system. Lack of sufficient information, however, precludes us from drawing any conclusions regarding the efficiency implications of sharecropping. We can only say that the high degree of uncertainty, which was a salient feature of Iranian farming, might have been a principal factor for the widespread occurrence of sharecropping in Iran.

Broadly speaking, the concentration of land in the hands of a few absentee landlords has been the key element in most criticisms of traditional tenancy systems. Therefore, the redistribution of land among the tenants has usually been considered to be a measure that would promote agricultural and rural development. We have argued, however, that this depends on whether a bimodal or a unimodal agrarian system emerges out of a land reform programme. The economic consequences of the two systems are quite different.

A unimodal agrarian sytem may follow a radical land redistribution programme and consists of family farms. Our analysis shows that this system would bring about an immediate income redistribution in favour of the majority of farmers and generate agricultural development. The essence of the argument is rather simple: the farmers have every incentive to use their resources, especially the abundant family labour, to increase their output and capital. Moreover, the important point is that the prevailing circumstances in a unimodal system as well as government policies would presumably encourage the peasants.

On the other hand, a land reform can redistribute only a limited amount of land but succeed in convincing the large landlords that they have to give up their traditional behaviour and become modern agriculturists. This leads to a bimodal agrarian system in which very small peasants coexist with large landowners. We maintain that the large landowners would enjoy both monopoly power in the market and government support and may increasingly use modern, imported technology. As a result, they would tend to become richer. On the contrary, the small peasants would fail to improve their situation because the imperfect markets and government policies often operate against them. They may eventually experience a fall in their standard of living.

The land reform experience in Iran exemplifies the latter case. As a consequence of the land reform programme which started in 1962 and of generally bimodal-oriented government policies, a bimodal system replaced the Iranian landlord–peasant system. The large farmers in post-reform agriculture owned a relatively large proportion of the arable land, had easier access to water and capital, and enjoyed government support. They were therefore encouraged to invest in capital-intensive methods and cultivate an increasing amount of cash crops. The growing of cash crops turned out to be more beneficial especially as a consequence of the government policy to control the price of wheat, which is the major staple crop in Iran.

In contrast to the large farmers, the Iranian small farmers generally owned small patches of land, often faced difficulties with respect to the irrigation water, and could hardly obtain sufficient credits. Moreover, no serious attempt was made to introduce follow-up programmes after the reform and the small farmers were practically deprived of government support. The small farmers had by and large little chance to improve their farming and their standards of living under the conditions which prevailed in Iranian agriculture after the land reform. They continued to cultivate the staple crops, largely by traditional methods. They produced these crops chiefly for their own consumption; nevertheless, the production of many of the peasants was insufficient to support their families.

There were also large numbers of landless labourers who were among the poor in the villages. They generally received no land under the land reform and their number in fact increased as some tenants were legally or illegally deprived of their rights to receive land. Decreasing agricultural employment opportunities as a result of the tendency towards mechanization among the large farmers in addition to poverty and small size of land on the part of peasants put further pressure on the rural labourers.

Sharp increases in oil income and the resulting urban boom might have come as a blessing for many poor people in the rural areas. The following mass migration to cities might have raised the well-being of those who left and reduced somewhat the pressures on those who did not. Nevertheless, only a small group of rural people experienced increasing improvements in their welfare and poverty remained the lot of the majority.

Glossary

arbab	landlord; master
barzigar	cultivator; the lowest member of a *buneh*
buneh	a team of peasants who grouped together to cultivate a specified amount of land
dang	one-sixth part of a village
iqta	land assignment; *tuyul*
juft	plough-land; an amount of land which is approximately between 4 to 6 hectares
khaliseh	state land
khwushnishin	a villager who did not have cultivation rights before the land reform; a landless villager
nasaq	a cultivation right of the village land before the land reform; the lay-out of a village lands
nasaqdar	a villager who had cultivation rights
pabuneh	an assistant of a *sarbuneh*
qanat	underground water channel
raiyat	a peasant who cultivated the land of a landlord in accordance with the local customs
sarbuneh	the head of a *buneh*
vaqf	land endowed for certain purposes, usually religious or charitable

Notes

Chapter 1   Introduction

1 In some cases, we had no access to the original statistics and had to rely on second-hand sources. If it is not stated to the contrary, even these statistics should be regarded as official.
2 For example, Research Group (1962), which studies the production of wheat and barley in Zanjan region, concludes that the statistics of the Ministry of Agriculture were extremely exaggerated for this region and prefers those of the Statistical Centre.
3 The reported number of villages varies greatly. At the beginning of the land reform in 1962 it was reported to be about 49,000 villages. Later reports give much higher figures. According to the 1973 agricultural census, there were 59,189 villages and 23,122 independent and attached farms. About 99 per cent of the rural population lived in the villages. See Ashraf (1979). See also Momeni (1980: 22–4) for a discussion about the number of villages.
4 For instance, most villages in the south-east and east of the country consist of two or three peasant families. On the other hand, in Azarbayjan, villages are much larger and often have several thousand people (Lambton 1969: 8–9).

Chapter 2   Agricultural backwardness in theory

1 It should be considered that since the end of the Second World War a great number of agrarian policies, especially land reform, have been adopted in many developing countries. As a consequence, agrarian systems in some of these countries might have changed partially or completely over the past four decades. See, for example, Dovring (1970), Warriner (1969) and King (1977).
2 There is little empirical evidence for notoriously high consumption propensities of landlords. For an attempt to provide such evidence for Latin America, see Stenberg (1970).
3 Nevertheless, sharing the crop might be seen as a risk-sharing device which can provide an incentive for a sharecropper to innovate. For further discussion, see pp. 19–22.

147

4 This is what Lipton (1968) calls the 'survival algorithm'. That is to say, poor farmers cannot afford a harvest failure, which means starvation or loss of land, and therefore focus on survival rather than profit under conditions of uncertainty. In other words, they avert from the risks which jeopardize their 'certain' subsistence harvest and thereby dispense with the expected risk premium. For further discussion see *ibid.* and Weeks (1970).

5 Johnson (1950) provides a brief summary of this traditional view about sharecropping and an expansion of this summary can be found in Cheung (1969).

6 For a fixed-rent tenant the rent is a fixed cost and his marginal cost will be equal to that of an owner-operator and his labour inputs for income maximization becomes equal, too.

7 Note that equation (2) is the core of inefficiency argument, i.e. tenants apply labour until their share of marginal products equals the wage rates.

8 Johnson emphasizes the last practice. Griffin (1976: 122), too, believes that insecurity of tenancy is in fact a means by which landlords are able to get rid of bad tenants who are not efficient.

9 In fact, Johnson accepts that theoretically sharecropping is less productive than fixed-rent tenancy although the two may be identical in practice (Cheung 1969: 49–51).

10 Cheung's landlord allows his tenant to receive only an income equal to his alternative wage earning. To maximize his income, the landlord divides his total land, s, equally among m tenants so that $H = s/m$ and his total rent is $y_1 = mrQ$. He then maximizes his income by choosing m, r, and L, subject to the constraint that each tenant receives $y_t = WL$. That is to say:

$$\text{Max } y_1 = mrF(H,L), \text{ subject to } WL = (1-r)F(H,L) \qquad \text{(I)}$$
$$(m,r,L)$$

Considering the fact that $H = s/m$, we get the following necessary conditions:

$$F_H = r\frac{Q}{H} \qquad \text{(II)}$$

$$F_L = W \qquad \text{(III)}$$

$$r = \frac{Q - WL}{Q} \qquad \text{(IV)}$$

We can see that equation (III), in contrast to equation (2), implies that sharecroppers apply labour as much as they otherwise would do.

11 Bardhan and Srinivasan (1971: 52) argue that an atomistic landlord in a competitive market takes r, which is determined in the market, as given. See also Koo (1973: 572).

12 Sen (1975: 67) also refers to this problem. He argues that it is one thing to stipulate the number of men who have to work in a piece of land, but it is quite another to specify the amount of labour hours to be applied, and still more complex to have a contract on the exact intensity of effort. See also Stiglitz (1974: 242–3) for further discussion of this problem.

13 Bardhan and Srinivasan (1971) assume that the tenant devotes part of his labour to the sharecropped land and sells part of it in the labour market at a given wage rate. The landlord also rents part of his land to sharecroppers and retains part which he cultivates with hired labour. The utility of each agent is then a function of his total income and his leisure.

14 This is a point which was initially brought up by Newbery (1974) who argues that Bardhan and Srinivasan's model shows that, at any rental share, peasants want to rent more and more land until its marginal utility falls to zero. This makes the demand for land exceed its supply.

15 In this system, there are three kinds of contracts, namely sharecropping, fixed-rent tenancy, and own cultivation with hired labour. Then the above assumption means that the tenant has to devote all his labour to work on the land he sharecrops and rents under fixed-rent tenancy, and what remains of his total labour has to be sold in the market. The landowner, in his turn, has to divide all his land between sharecropped land, fixed-rented land, and own-cultivation.

16 The total gain is L_1JBL_2 which is greater than the landlord's total cost L_1ACL_2. It is also greater than the wage cost to the tenant, L_1ABL_2.

17 On incentive creating features of sharecropping, see further Stiglitz (1974: 242–51) and Reid (1977: 405).

18 Accordingly, Lucas compares the two systems with Cobb-Douglas production functions, separable utility functions, and a linear monitoring cost function. He finds out that, 'the share-cum-wage economy is . . . technically efficient in the sense of equating marginal products of factors in both uses' (Lucas 1979: 519).

19 At the same time, Johnson admits that the data were very rough and the lands rented under the two lease systems were not proved to be comparable (Johnson 1950: 118).

20 Provided that the sharecropper alone stands for all the costs, as is normal in many traditional rural economies. Adam Smith (1937: 367) puts the above argument in this way: 'It could never, however, be the interest [of the sharecroppers] to lay out in the further improvement of the land any part of the little stock which they might have saved from their own share of produce, because the lord, who laid out nothing, was to get one-half of whatever it produced.'

21 We should recall that Cheung's sharecropper (see p. 13) is satisfied with receiving his alternative wage earning and is passive in decision making. The landlord, however, makes sure that the tenant receives his wage-equivalent share anyhow. Such a tenant would hardly use and take care of the new investments properly without some extra supervision costs.

22 Bardhan and Srinivasan conclude further that such a tenant would prefer the landlord not to share costs if he had the choice (Bardhan and Srinivasan 1971: 61–2).

23 In fact, Bell (1976: 183, 188) concludes that a landlord is more likely to prefer a cost-sharing: (i) the higher the rental share, (ii) the larger the returns to scale in all inputs combined, (iii) the more risk averse his tenant relative to himself, and (iv) the greater the production risks.

24 In a rich economy, y_{ms} is likely to be substantially above y_{mp}, reflecting mainly an average Q which is much greater than y_{mp}. As the risk of falling below y_{mp} or y_{ms} becomes very small, a tenant would try mainly to attain his desired income level, y_D. He is ready to bear more risk to increase his chance of achieving this income level. A fixed-rent contract provides such an opportunity and is thus more attractive.

25 There are also several models which try to explain the occurrence of sharecropping mainly on the basis of transaction costs. See, for example, Agrawal (1984) and Pertev (1986) who focus on supervision costs.

26 For example, Newbery (1977) argues that production decisions in agriculture are affected by various unforeseen events during a crop year. This will affect the demand for labour over the year in a random way and thus the labour market cannot guarantee full employment at a constant, or even predictable, wage rate. It is then plausible to assume that wage rates are risky and equal to $w\phi(s)$ because the state of the world, s, is not known. He then introduces this factor first in a system where only fixed-rent tenancy is available and, then, in a system where both fixed-rent tenancy and sharecropping are available. He finds out that only the latter system is efficient.

27 Family labour cannot, or will not, always move away from the family farms for a variety of reasons: they may simply prefer to work on the family farm, they may be forbidden by custom to accept outside work, as is the case for women and children in some places, they may be ready to work part-time but restrained by the problem of location, etc. See further Mazumdar (1975: 261–4), Bardhan (1973: 1379–81), and Sen (1975: 53–5).

28 In other words, the area WEA = the area ABC. We should remember that the landlords in Cheung model stipulate a minimum labour input at L_2. See p. 13.

Chapter 3   Pre-reform Iranian village

1 This was an important land category before the seventh century but, for a variety of reasons, such as the increase of land assignment, commendation and usurpation, its volume decreased sharply. For more details see Nomani (1980: 174–87).

2 In fact, it was not until the eleventh century that land assignment became the dominant type of landholding under the name of *iqta*.

Notes

Later, the term was gradually replaced by *tuyul*. See Lambton (1953: 28) and Nomani (1980: 201–28).

3 Theoretically, *khaliseh* (crown land) and *divani* (state domains) were different. The income of the former was supposed to finance the expenses of the court while that of the latter was supposed to be spent by government for the whole society (Nomani 1980: 151–74). In practice, they were not really distinguishable. In modern usage *khaliseh* is state domains and *amlak*, the crown estates. See pp. 32–3.

4 This process began when 'The need for more money to pay for extravagances of the court, to provide for administration of the country and the upkeep of the army, became ever more pressing in the latter part of the Qajar period' (Lambton 1953: 151).

5 Since the 1930s several laws passed which dealt with these lands: in 1937 for the sale of *khaliseh* around Tehran, and Sistan, in 1947 for *khaliseh* in Khuzestan, and in 1955 for the sale of state domains in general. See Lambton (1953: 240–55), Homan (1955: 286–97), and Denman (1978: 260–2).

6 Land property was expressed in terms of villages and parts of villages in Iran. Each village consisted of six equal parts, regardless of its size, and each part was called a *dang*. There were further subdivisions, as well.

7 Lambton (1953: 269–71) reports the results of an unpublished study which showed that the areas with higher average annual rainfall coincided with a higher degree of land concentration.

8 It is worth noting that there were other landlords who owned shares in different villages and were called small-owners, but were virtually large landowners if one considers the sum of their shares. In official statistics such large landowners, small-owners, and peasant proprietors are all called *khordeh malekin*, and therefore it is difficult to estimate the amount of land that smallholders owned. However, *khordeh malekin*, i.e. those with less than one *dang* in any one village, owned 42 per cent of villages (Kazemi and Abrahamian 1978: 269).

9 There are, however, great variations in the estimates of state domains. See, for example, Ashraf and Banuazizi (1980: 18) and Azkia (1986: 86).

10 Although theoretically a *vaqf* cannot be dissolved and thus usurped, there have been numerous cases of usurpation of such lands throughout history. Consequently, to endow lands as personal *vaqfs* was not always a safe protection against usurpation. See Nomani (1980: 189–91) and Lambton (1953: 131–2) for some examples.

11 It should be emphasized that all four land categories described in the foregoing section were used in rather similar ways. In state and endowed lands the renters or administrators acted as the landlords and followed the same fashion.

12 For discussion about sharecropping as a risk-sharing device, see Chapter 2, pp. 19–22).

13 A section of the Civil Code deals with sharecropping. However, the law approaches such contracts very generally and it mainly legalizes the system rather than trying to unify practices. An English translation of this section can be found in Lambton (1953: 402–4).

151

14 Saedloo (1979: 781–98) who discusses the inheritance issue in the villages in detail concludes that other heirs virtually benefited from the right as long as they lived in the family. If anyone of them left, he would receive a share of annual product even though it was sometimes very small.

15 There were also other common terms for plough-lands. The same is true for most of the terms used in this study. The terms used here should only be considered as the more common ones in the rural study literature.

16 In less fertile regions, and especially in peasant proprietor areas, and where ploughing was done by spade, the village holdings were reckoned by reference to a share of water. In such cases, the village water was divided in a varying number of shares of equal duration in time which could be used for irrigation (Lambton 1953: 7).

17 A headman is quoted to have said: 'Every year we must go to the landlord at harvest time and give him gifts for the opportunity of cultivating his land for next year. . . . Owners throw out gavband [group-farming] members at their slightest whim. If one of us forgets to say "Good morning" to the landlord he would throw us off the land' (Keddie 1972: 382). See also Azkia (1980: 32).

18 For a detailed list of the various tasks of the members of each *buneh*, see Safinezhad (1972: 46–9). Lambton (1953: 299–302) provides some examples of such tasks in several areas. Generally, a hierarchy existed within each *buneh*, *sarbunehs* at the top and *barzigars* on the bottom, and the hard tasks were pushed downward. See Safinezhad (1972: 30).

19 For more information about *qanats* see Chapter. 1, pp. 5–6.

20 For a discussion about sharecropping and the incentive question, see Chapter 2, pp. 11–15.

21 For example, one can see an extensive list of different practices in Lambton (1953: 308–29). See also Research Group (1965a: 116–20).

22 The importance of such problems are studied, among others, by Lambton (1953: 157–60, 283–94), Abrahamian (1975: 140–7), and Nomani (1980: 451–71).

23 For example in Semirom and Daran where spring water is used, a farmer who supplied the oxen, labour, manure and seed got about four-fifths of the wheat while a similar farmer received between a third to a half of the crop in Yazd, where the water is obtained from long deep *qanats* (Research Group 1965: 119). Reviewing the division of the crop in the province of Kerman, Lambton (1953: 312) concludes that the share of the peasant was considerably less than in most areas which was partly due to the heavy maintenance expenses of the very lengthy *qanats*.

24 It should be noted that rice was usually cultivated on a fixed-rent basis, in cash or in kind. See Lambton (1953: 321–2).

25 Soodagar (1978: 134) believes that two other factors strengthened the position of such sharecroppers. These crops required more skilled labour, and they were usually grown around towns by more socially conscious farmers.

26 The extra dues and their effects on peasant income is discussed later, see p. 44.

27 Safinezhad (1972: 30) shows that in some places the annual income of a *sarbuneh* was about 5 to 12 per cent, and that of a *pabuneh* was about 2 to 3 per cent higher than a *barzigar's* income. In some cases the share of the group subdivided equally but the group cultivated a small piece of land whose income accrued exclusively to the *sarbuneh*, or *barzigars* worked one day a year free for him (Lambton 1953: 299; Khosrovi 1979b: 79–80).

28 There are striking similarities between the cultivation methods that historians, travellers, etc., described centuries ago with what were in use in 1950s. For example, see Nomani (1980: 293–325).

29 These were what a government company bought and sold to farmers between 1952 and 1962 but we don't know how many of them were in use by 1962. Some tractors had been imported before but only 240 of them were in service by 1955 (Adibi 1955: 132).

30 It can be seen from Table 3.4 that machinery was concentrated in Mazandaran, where commercial farming was growing. In fact, a sluggish movement towards mechanization was under way before the land reform. This was much more rapid in the 1950s when machines were bought to cultivate the idle lands and pastures. This occurred particularly in the highly fertile plain of Gorgan in Mazandaran province. Most of the lands in this province were crown lands and it was the royal family members, and some other upper class entrepreneurs from capital who were developing mechanized farms here. See further Okazaki (1968) and Nikayin (1976: 78–80).

31 For detailed description of various tools used for cultivation see Wulff (1966: 260–77).

32 It is estimated that a medium length *qanat* of about 9.5 km required $13,500–34,000 for construction and 0.5 per cent of that for maintenance (Wulff 1966: 254). At the same time, different estimates show that a peasant's family annual income, on average, might have been between $100 and $250 (Platt 1970: 24–5).

33 Around Esfahan, towers were made to collect pigeon droppings which were used as manure for fruit trees. For further details see Wulff (1965: 269–70).

34 Many examples of traditional practices and beliefs can be found in an old agricultural handbook reproduced by Yavari (1981: 95–167). See also Bolukbashi (1981).

35 For more examples about advantages of some traditional practices, see Siyahpoosh (1981).

36 On the other hand, Bharier (1971: 133–4) shows that several major crops increased fairly well between 1925 and 1959, and the increase in the production of wheat, for instance, might have matched the population increase. He concludes, however, that 'most of the production increases were the result of extending the area of cultivation rather than of using more intensive methods'.

37 This was mainly true for villages on the borders of the central desert. For example, one study (OIPFG 1974) shows that some of the villages of Kerman, a province in the neighbourhood of the central desert,

depended almost entirely upon rug and carpet weaving. See also Khosrovi (1979b: 133).

38 Remember that a plough-land, or *juft*, was between 4 to 6 hectares. See p. 35 for further information.

39 For further information about different dues, see Lambton (1953: 333−5) and Momeni (1980: 48−9).

40 In fact, agricultural labourers comprised more than 80 per cent of the *khwushnishins* who were the villagers without cultivation rights. Shop-keepers, money-lenders, village artisans, bathkeepers, etc., constituted the rest of the *khwushnishin* population. It is believed that around 40 per cent of Iran's rural population were *khwushnishins*. However, the proportion of *khwushnishins* to all villagers varied greatly from village to village. In general, a greater percentage of the population were *khwushnishins* in the larger villages and a lesser percentage in the smaller ones. For further information see Hooglund (1973 and 1982: 28−34).

41 The author, however, argues that these figures might have been unusually low (Keddie 1968: 71−2).

42 Lambton (1953: 389) describes the common diets of a peasant very accurately: 'The main feature of his diet apart from bread is *abgusht*, or soup, made chiefly by boiling a little meat with split peas and occasionally with some other pulses. In summer, he supplements his diet in the fruit growing areas with fruit and vegetables such as cucumber. If he owns flocks he also eats a small quantity of cheese and curds.'

43 There were some governmental institutions which provided agricultural credit such as the Agricultural Bank of Iran and the Rural Fund. The limited loans of these institutions were mainly received by landlords (Lambton 1953: 380; Platt 1970: 30).

44 For example, the reports of Research Group (1965a, 1970b) show that between 2 and 23 per cent of loans were received from landlords.

45 Kazemi and Abrahamian (1978: 275−80) argue that, apart from the communication problems, lack of enough surplus to sell and thus of income to consume, the need for irrigation, linguistic, religious and ethnic differences, periodic attacks by nomadic tribesmen, and the landlords' efforts to perpetuate the insularity of the villages encouraged the communal solidarity within the villages and discouraged the villagers from integrating into the market economy.

46 Lodi (1965: 1) believes that by preharvest selling the peasants avoided the risk of a price fall at harvest time, as well.

Chapter 4 Theoretical analysis of land reform

1 For instance, land registration might be described as land reform since it is useful to know how land is owned, it paves the way for subsequent reforms, etc. But, as far as rural poverty and inequality is concerned, it is absurd to call such measures land reform when they hardly affect the

way of life in rural areas. See further Warriner (1969: xiv–xv) and Lipton (1974: 269–74).

2 It should be noted that in arid regions, water is the determining factor for cultivation. For example, the previous chapter indicated that in many parts of Iran land without water is worthless. It is therefore better to measure land 'in "efficiency units" (indicating its capacity to yield net-value-added per acre in conjunction with optimal hirings of non-land inputs) rather than in crude acres' (Lipton 1974: 272).

3 As is discussed below, land reform involves important economic, social and political changes and requires a favourable socio-political climate. In the absence of favourable conditions, 'substitute measures' which have considerably less impact on the status quo become attractive as alternatives. See Lipton (1974: 274–81) and Flores (1970: 896–8) for discussion about the reliability of such measures as alternatives in practice.

4 For further discussion about the politics of land reform see, among others, Warriner (1969: Ch. 1 and 3); Layman and French (1970); and Huntington (1970).

5 For different examples, see Bergmann (1977: 19–21), Huntington (1970: 385–7); Gittinger (1961); and Ashraf and Banuazizi (1980: 27).

6 Cheung (1969: 100–17) argues that even certain kinds of government policies cause displacement of the already efficiently allocated resources and will lead to inefficiency.

7 Since the two systems correspond to what Johnston and Kilby (1975: 127–81) describe as the outcomes of 'unimodal' and 'bimodal' strategies of agrarian change, we also call the two systems 'unimodal' and 'bimodal'. Cf. Dovring (1970: 2–4).

8 As Griffin (1974: 22) writes, 'there is a spectrum along which landowner-ship or various sizes of farms will be distributed. . . . Nevertheless, it simplifies thought to imagine for the moment that farms are owned either by big landlords or by small peasants.'

9 The following two sections are largely based on Griffin (1974: 17–61).

10 There might be more than one large landowner in each local market who may then behave as collusive oligopolists (Lundahl 1984: 524).

11 For more details about price determination under these circumstances, see Lundahl (1984: Appendix).

12 For more information see Chapter 2, pp. 23–4, where labour-market dualism is explained.

13 It seems that many of the high-yielding seeds are of this nature because their applications are connected with other inputs which require capital. In fact, such innovations are packages of complementary changes. See Griffin (1974: 51–61), and Lundahl (1979: 582–5).

14 As was explained in Chapter 2, p. 10, poorer peasants may be more risk averse simply because they are poor and vulnerable to output varia-tions. This may lead some policy makers to conclude that poorer peasants are 'tradition bound', 'conservative', and 'change resistant' (Weeks 1970: 32).

15 De Janvry (1981: 169–72) provides an explanation for the bias of government policies based on the political power of large landlords.

16 Ghose (1983: 4) argues that growing landlessness and declining levels of rural employment and rural wages in developing countries may reduce the effective demand for food in rural areas. This can reduce, or even outweigh, the demand-pull which tends to raise food prices.

17 This is largely in line with the traditional view of sharecropping. As a sharecropper becomes an owner-operator, he will have no reason to work less intensively than L_2 in terms of Figure 2.1. Then, not only total agricultural output but also employment increases.

18 Berry's and Cline's estimate of the potential output gains from such a land reform in six developing countries shows that even in Asian countries, where farms are predominantly small, total production can rise. Such an increase is estimated to be, for example, 19 per cent in India and 10 per cent in the Philippines (Berry and Cline 1979: 132–3).

19 Multiple cropping is a prominent example. Dorner (1972: 105) writes that the change from single to double cropping of rice raised the demand for labour by 80 per cent in Chekiang Province in China; the change from double to triple cropping increased labour requirements up to two or three times that of double cropping in Taiwan.

20 In cases where timely ploughing by tractors makes double cropping possible, or where tractors enable farmers to plough hard soil which otherwise would not be used, tractors are complementary with labour (Griffin 1974: 53). See also Misawa (1974: 322–4).

21 It is even possible that, under certain circumstances, land reform affects the non-land recipient adversely. In the final analysis, the post-reform situation of these people will largely depend on the changes in the demand for hired labour in the agricultural sector. See further Berry (1971).

22 As Lipton (1974: 296) points out, the situation will be different in Latin America where most landless labourers, without knowledge and experience in farming, might get land. The need for some follow-up is acute in such a case.

23 Even when it becomes necessary to hire a labourer now and then, he would in most circumstances need very little supervision, as his work is controlled by family members who are already in the workplace (Pertev 1986: 33).

24 For further information about these features of sharecropping see Chapter 2, pp. 22–3.

Chapter 5   An analysis of the Iranian land reform programme

1 For example, it is estimated that the televisions and cars which were stored in Iran in 1960 could meet the local demand of these goods for four years (Momeni 1980: 177).

2 The programme was suggested by the IMF and the World Bank as a

precondition for helping the country. See Mahdavy (1965: 135–6) and Bharier (1971: 95).

3 For a very good and well-documented survey of different views with respect to the agrarian question in Iran see Momeni (1980: 81–118, 206–11). See also Hooglund (1982: 36–48).

4 The above decrees were issued by the government of Dr Musaddiq in October 1952. His government, which was supported by a vast majority of people, was overthrown in a coup in August 1953. For further information about this period, see Cottam (1964).

5 The Soviet Union and her allies were broadcasting 132 hours of criticism per month toward Iran and there were three clandestine radio stations sending out anti-regime programmes (Ashraf and Banuazizi 1980: 26). See also Lambton (1969: 61).

6 In 1959, the then US Senator Hubert Humphrey said: 'I think there are revolutionary forces at work in Iran, and I think those forces are at work in the tribes and villages' (Ashraf and Banuazizi 1980: 27). In fact, Americans were convinced that land reform was necessary in Iran and insisted that Iranians should introduce a reform programme (Ashraf and Banuazizi 1980: 27; Fishburne 1964: 162–3, 264–74).

7 It is estimated that 50 to 60 per cent of the members of the parliaments were from the landowning class (Ajami 1973: 122).

8 See Momeni (1980: 144–52) for some information on the proposed bill and the passed law. See also Lambton (1969: 56–8) and Khatibi (1972: 63–4).

9 Quoted from Arsanjani, the Minister of Agriculture, in a press conference, where he gave information about a new land reform law in 1962. See p. 72.

10 It was normally both houses of parliaments, the *Majlis* and the Senate, which were to pass laws but, as we mentioned above, they had already been dissolved. For an English translation of the land reform law of January 1962 see *Iran Almanac* (1962).

11 Only charitable *vaqfs* were exempted while personal *vaqfs* were treated as other private lands whose beneficiaries were able to receive the revenue of a maximum of one village. For information about *vaqfs*, see Chapter 3, p. 32.

12 The Land Reform Council was under the chairmanship of the Minister of Agriculture and consisted of four high officials of the Ministry of Agriculture and the director of the Land Reform Organization. The interpretation of the reform law and drawing up the regulations were among the duties of this council. See Research Group (1970a: 49, 52).

13 The 36th session of the Land Reform Council, 18 December 1962.

14 The decisions were taken in the 43rd (7 June 1963) and 47th (25 August 1963) sessions of the Land Reform Council. In fact, the 43rd session decided that 'women landowners, in the same way as men and irrespective of their position in the household, are entitled to upper legal limit of land' (Research Group 1970a: 54–5). This practically implied that the wife (and perhaps the wives?) were entitled to retain one whole village.

15 This decision (on 28 January 1963) was in line with land reform officials who had not allowed landlords to choose such villages. See Research Group (1970a: 58).
16 The session of the Council on 24 July 1963 (Lambton 1969: 67).
17 The first decision was made at the 25th session in early months and the second decision was made at the 39th session on 18 March 1963.
18 The regional indices were between 100 and 180. For a detailed list of indices, see Denman (1973: 340–1).
19 According to the law, if a beneficiary fails to pay three of his annual instalments, his land could be confiscated by the government and sold to another. The law does not state anything about the repayment of the already paid instalments (Research Group 1970a: 67).
20 According to Lambton (1969: 206) oral instructions were given to the land reform officials not to allow the sale of the cultivation rights.
21 Notification was given to the landlords in Maragheh to declare their holding on 16 January. See further Land (1965: 100) and Lambton (1969: 87).
22 The Land Reform Organization began its activity with only twenty officials in 1962 (Lambton 1969: 99).
23 Such peasants felt that it was unfair to exclude them from the benefits of the reform. Disputes arose since many of these peasants refused to pay the landlords' share of the crops. See Lambton (1969: 104, 192) and Momeni (1980: 234–5).
24 The first draft of these regulations was issued on 7 February 1963 but underwent substantial amendments before it was passed by the *Majlis* and the Senate. See further Lambton (1969: 104–8, 194–215). For an English translation of the Additional Articles and the original draft of the regulations for their execution see also *Iran Almanac* (1963).
25 It was not clear whether the peasant had to pay two-fifths of the value of the total land before division or two-fifths of the value of the land which the peasant received; the text could be read either way (Lambton 1969: 203).
26 In both cases, the Agricultural Credit and Rural Development Bank paid one-third of the price directly to the landlord on behalf of the peasant (Momeni 1980: 237). For more details, see Lambton (1969: 201–4).
27 The draft articles for the third stage were submitted to the parliament in September 1968 and was finally approved on 13 January 1969. See Momeni (1980: 239), and Hooglund (1982: 69–70). An English translation of this law could be found in *Iran Almanac* (1969).
28 Instead of paying in cash, the peasant could pay the price of land in twelve annual instalments. In such a case, the price would be two-fifths of twelve annual rents minus 15 per cent.
29 This was called 'exchange for the better'. See Lambton (1969: 106).
30 It was estimated that a cadastral survey of all villages would have taken thirty years and would have cost about 64 million dollars (Momeni 1980: 151–2).
31 In some cases, for example, the land reform officials in practice found a

quantitative formula for mechanization. They gave farm improvement practices and machinery specific points; for example, a tractor got 10 points, discs 10, a combine 15, use of chemical fertilizers 5. A landlord who scored 51 points or more was judged to have 'mechanized' his land (Denman 1973: 104).

32 Jacoby (1971: 199) believes that one of the main reasons for the success of the Japanese land reform was the active role of the peasants in its implementation.

33 Of course, the abortive law of 1960 served as a warning to landlords and they had two years to sell their lands, transfer their villages to their wives or children, etc., and some exercised such practices (Keddie 1968: 82; Momeni 1980: 153–6). But there were many who did not react even to the news of a forthcoming land reform law, because they hardly believed that such laws could be put into operation. They supposed that the measure would be forgotten like so many other measures before it (Lambton 1969: 63).

34 According to the regulations of the second stage the landlords were allowed to take any action with respect to their land until the date that the execution of the law would begin, provided that they held the land legally. This was in contradiction to the provisions of the first stage which prohibited any transaction from the date of the passing of the law. See Momeni (1980: 237).

35 The unaffected lands were the retained lands, gardens and fruit orchards, *vaqf* lands, and lands of 'petty landowners'.

36 If the laws and regulations are supposed to be passed by a parliament or parliaments, they will be put into operation after they are passed. The parliament(s) can then influence the land reform as well.

37 Zonis (1971: 158–9) provides interesting information about land-holdings of the political elite in Iran.

38 In July 1962, Alam succeeded Amini as prime minister.

39 Arsanjani was succeeded on 12 March 1963 by General Riahi, whose deputy minister was a colonel. Arsanjani left the impression that he might have favoured a more radical second stage (Mahadvy 1965: 139). See also Momeni (1980: 283–4).

40 By September 1963 the number of land reform officials had increased to 1,184 Lambton (1969: 99).

41 Examples of such a point of view could be found in Saedloo (1972) and Doroudian (1976).

42 It should be noted that according to the land reform law of 1962 barren lands of the villages were to be acquired by the government for redistribution. In 1963, the Land Reform Council decided to postpone the sale of these lands. In 1965, the government offered these lands to interested developers at a price fixed by the government. Finally, the government offered these lands free of charge and provided financial help for their developers. See further Lambton (1969: 78–80) and Denman (1973: 154–8).

43 The law was passed in 1967.

44 A new type of farm corporation was also established by the government

from the early 1970s. They were called 'production co-operatives' and differed from corporations in two main respects: (a) the farmers retained their title to their lands, and (b) they were guaranteed a position in team works that cultivated the co-operative land. See Azkia (1980: 135–7).

45 The minimum of 51 per cent of votes was required for the establishment of a corporation. Calculating percentages to ascertain the extent of the majority was not done village by village but over the entire selected region. A village might then be included into a farm corporation contrary to the wishes of the majority (Denman 1973: 213).

46 Lambton (1969: 316) writes: 'Almost universally the peasants expected the cooperative societies to provide first loans and secondly water by wells or other means.'

Chapter 6   The agrarian system after the land reform

1 This was announced by Arsanjani, the Minister of Agriculture, in a press conference on 15 January 1962. He also revealed that a small group of experts from his department had been working to prepare the execution of the land reform in this region since October 1961. See also Land (1965/6: 100).

2 The local Democrat government which was in power in Azarbayjan between 1945 and 1946 adopted a land reform measure. Although this government was overthrown, its land reform stopped, and the land-lords largely regained their land, the landlord–peasant relationship was considerably weakened. See Lambton (1969: 36–7) and Hooglund (1982: 41–2).

3 According to Article 8 of the land reform law the landlords had to declare their landholdings within about forty days after the first announcement which showed that the government intended to begin the land reform in a given area.

4 The difference is in fact slightly higher than Table 6.1 shows since the number of redistributed villages in the first period, i.e. 8,042, comprise only private villages redistributed, while the figures for the other two periods, i.e. 8,109 and 666, include state and perhaps crown villages as well. The progress made between January 1962 and September 1963 is more comparable with the total number of villages redistributed in the first stage which is given in Table 6.3, because it excludes state villages. See Denman (1978: 267), Salour (1963: 58), and Statistical Centre of Iran (1966, 1971).

5 The order is based on information in Lambton (1953: 270–1) which shows that, in general, there was a positive relationship between large landlordism and land fertility.

6 There are also reports of such an exercise. For example, Lambton (1969: 259) writes that landowners in Kermanshah deliberately selected parts of different villages with the object of retaining their influence over a wider area. She writes further that even landlords in Kordistan

intended to use this method but were discouraged by the land reform officials.

7 For a discussion about the definition of mechanized land in the law, see Chapter 5, pp. 77–8).

8 A study (OIPFG 1974: 42) points out that some women from a village which was exempted because of 'mechanization' believed that mechanization implied that one received a certain amount of wheat and money instead of sharing the crop. See also Lambton (1969: 101).

9 Warriner (1969: 123) writes that this method was widely used in Tehran and to a lesser extent in Esfahan.

10 Lambton (1969: 262), for instance, points to such cases in Arak and Esfahan.

11 See also Lambton (1969: 258) and Momeni (1980: 291) for other examples.

12 A number of such attempts can be found in Momeni (1980: 287–92).

13 We have assumed that the total number of Iranian villages was 60,000. For more information, see Chapter 1, p. 4.

14 About 3,000 out of a total 8,042 villages were entire villages, and the rest were equivalent to 2,520 entire villages. Thus, around 5,520 entire villages had been purchased by this date.

15 We have used the statistics of the public census of 1956 (Ministry of Interior 1961) for this purpose. It is safe to use these statistics since the number of those with cultivation rights, who were eligible to receive land, could only have slightly increased from that date until the start of the reform and because no account is taken of the *khwushnishin* population. See Chapter 3, p. 35.

16 The percentage is based on the number of rural families in 1966, i.e. 3 million families. Case studies and sporadic reports about land redistribution substantiate our conclusion that even 19 per cent is a generous percentage (Land 1965/6: 105; Momeni 1980: 313–14). As a matter of fact, a simple calculation reveals the likely exaggeration of the official statistics as well as our estimate. The official statistics indicate that the Iranian villages have on the average about 250 inhabitants or roughly 50 families, including *khwushnishins*. See, for example, Ministry of Interior (1961: 21) and Khosrovi (1979b: 9). Provided that the total number of six-*dang* villages which redistributed in the first stage is 9,514, Table 6.3 and our estimate indicate that each redistributed village had on average 75 and 60 households respectively, excluding the *khwushnishins*.

17 For further information about these five alternatives, see Chapter 5, pp. 74–6.

18 Both Lambton (1969: 217) and Hooglund (1982: 65–6) point out that there were notable exceptions.

19 See further Momeni (1980: 262–3) and OIPFG (1973: 60–1). In addition to the differences in the official figures, the implicit assumption in the data of the second stage that each landowner had only one estate is in all probability wrong. There might have been landowners who had small estates, for example, in different villages. Cf. Table 72 in

Bank Markazi Iran, *Annual Report and Balance Sheet* (1966: 135) and a similar table in Lambton (1969: 221).

20 Report issued by the land reform organization in 1966 indicates that 828 six-*dang* villages were claimed to be mechanized and another 1,405 villages were declared to be wholly gardens. See Lambton (1969: 221).

21 A study (Salmanzadeh and Jones 1979: 121) shows that in Dezful, in the Khuzestan Province, about 5 per cent of those who received land by division were second-time beneficiaries.

22 A table in Momeni *ibid* shows that a large majority of landlords declared their preference for division. Although the figures are different, this might be the result of the above mentioned inquiry in Denman (1973: 145).

23 We could either argue that similar to the second stage, those landlords who received a larger share of the crop under the sharecropping system chose to divide their land or assume that in the division cases the land was shared equally between landlords and peasants. However, the difference is insignificant.

24 See note 5 above.

25 There is evidence which suggests that *vaqf* land was not always transferred to the peasants but was sometimes usurped by influential civil servants and military officials. See Momeni (1980: 300−1).

26 See Denman (1973: 81) and *Iran Almanac* (1973: 395). We have assumed that all 491 crown villages (out of 1008) which remained outstanding in 1962 were sold to the peasants. For more information about the sale of state and crown land see Chapter 3, pp. 29, 33.

27 The remnants of the old tenure systems are discussed later in this chapter.

28 For instance McLachlan's (1968: 687) estimate shows that large landowners' landed properties covered about 56 per cent of the total agricultural land although they owned less than 35 per cent of all villages.

29 See a list of examples in Platt (1970: 77) which is extracted from Lambton (1969: Chs 6, 7, and 8), Momeni (1980: 314−15) and Azkia (1986: 123−4).

30 For more examples see also Khosrovi (1982), and Azkia (1986: 120−7).

31 See also Momeni (1980: 343) and Azkia (1980: 122) for other forms of sharecropping.

32 In fact Khosrovi (1982: 43) calls the owners of these farms medium landowners rather than rich peasants.

33 Khosrovi (1982: 43) writes that holdings of 30 to 50 hectares were principally concentrated in Azarbayjan, Bushehr, Gilan, Hamadan, Kermanshah, Kordestan, Khuzestan and Zanjan.

34 Some basic information about all fifteen large agribusinesses is provided in Momeni (1980: 354).

35 Hooglund (1982: 86−7) mentions that there were two corporations which consisted of one single village each and, on the other hand, an exceptionally large corporation with forty-five villages.

36 For more information about the main features of the law governing establishment of farm corporation see Chapter 5, p. 84.

37 Difficulties of the small farmers with respect to irrigation will be discussed in more detail in the next chapter.

Chapter 7 Economic consequences of the land reform

1 For example, the available data reveals that 83 and 87 per cent of all the irrigation expenditures in 1968 and 1969, respectively, was spent on such projects. See Bank Markazi Iran, *Annual Report and Balance Sheet* (1969, 1971). Cf. Azkia (1980: 96).
2 It was mentioned in Chapter 4 (see p. 50) that because of the importance of water in agriculture in arid regions, land should be measured in 'efficiency units'. This would reflect the differences in fertility of land caused by the differences in the availability of water.
3 The Agricultural Development Bank of Iran was established in 1968 under the name of the Agricultural Development Fund of Iran. Its name and some of its regulations were changed in 1973.
4 Katouzian (1974: 233) has estimated that even after the peasants received government credits in 1970 and 1971 their income deficit for each year was about 59 and 73 billion rials, respectively.
5 Unfortunately we do not know much about the credits which different government agencies provided. We know that these credits were given for regional development programmes growing special crops such as tea and sugar, or sale of machinery (Aresvik 1976: 172). As we will discuss later in this chapter, it was predominantly large farmers who cultivated such crops and used machinery. Therefore, we can assume that these farmers might have benefited most from such credits as well.
6 Interest rates on state loans to corporations ranged from 2 to 8 per cent but they could pay only 1 per cent interest and reinvest the rest (Katouzian 1983: 332–3).
7 A small number of these loans, which were probably obtained from relatives and friends, were free of charge. See Khosrovi (1979b: 163).
8 This does not include 600,000 workers, i.e. 11 per cent of the rural labour force, who were only seasonally unemployed. See Statistical Centre of Iran (1984: 61, 78).
9 Mechanized land was even exempted from the reform in the first stage. However, there were two differences: (1) the second stage clearly defined mechanized land and (2) most landlords who were subject to the second stage were in practice 'smaller' landlords who might have needed to prove that their land was mechanized while the bigger, more influential landlords might not. For further information about the regulations of the second stage see Chapter 5, pp. 74–5.
10 We should consider further that Kordestan and West Azarbayjan were among the regions which had proportionately a large number of 10–50 hectare farms, i.e. medium-sized farms and the lower strata of large farms; see Khosrovi (1981: 40).
11 These five provinces were Esfahan, Gilan, Khorasan, Mazandaran and

Markazi which consumed, respectively, 16, 11, 9, 21 and 17 per cent of all fertilizers in 1971.

12 Rice was in fact a semi-cash crop. It was the dominant staple food crop in the rice-growing provinces, namely Gilan and Mazandaran. At the same time, it was a comparatively profitable cash crop for many peasants.

13 In 1975 the net income of each hectare of land under pistachio and citrus fruits was, respectively, eight times and twice that of rice (Khosrovi 1979: 105). At the same time, the net income of one hectare of land under rice was four times the net income of one hectare of land under wheat (Azkia 1986: 168). See also Rafipoor (1985: 199–200).

14 Okazaki (1969: 28) writes that numerous large farms appeared in Mazandaran with the main purpose of cotton production.

15 In fact, the wheat purchase of the Cereals Organization in some years was 0.1 per cent, or even less, of total production. See Aresvik (1976: 144, Table 7.6).

16 Hakimian (1988) argues that many of the agricultural output changes in Iran were in fact a result of the rural–urban migration caused by non-agricultural higher wages.

Chapter 8   Rural poverty and inequality after the reform

1 The main problem with the above estimate is that it ignores the fact that some of these small farmers are rice-growers and orchardgrowers: the latter presumably do not produce wheat and the former principally cultivate and consume rice. Although this will change the estimated percentages it does not change the above conclusion.

2 Another study (Katouzian 1983: 343–4) shows that the share of the poorest rural households in total expenditures increased slightly at the expense of the richest between 1967 and 1972, but concludes that the developments since 1972 lead one to believe that the distribution of rural expenditures, and income, might have worsened in subsequent years. See also Pesaran (1976: 280).

3 Azkia (1980: 253) shows that the peasants' debts in two regions trebled between 1969 and 1978. See also Katouzian (1974: 233) and Azkia (1986: 152).

4 For some information about the corporations after the Revolution see Azkia (1986: 252–5) and a Group of Experts (1980: 46–57).

5 However, undernourishment was more widespread in the urban areas while severe undernourishment was more common in the rural areas (Katouzian 1983: 348).

Bibliography

Abrahamian, E. (1975) 'European feudalism and Middle Eastern despotisms', *Science and Society*, vol. 39.

Adams, D.W. (1973) 'The economics of land reform', *Food Research Institute Studies*, vol. 12.

Adams, D.W. and Rask, N. (1968) 'Economics of cost-share leases in less developed countries, *American Journal of Agricultural Economics*, vol. 50.

Abidi, M. (1955) 'Measure Pre-requisite to the Development of Land and Water in Iran', unpublished dissertation, Colombia University.

Agah Book Collection (1982) *Masā'il- arẓi va dihgāni-yi Irān va Khāvarmiyāneh* [Agrarian and peasant problems of Iran and the Middle East], Tehran: Agah Publications.

Agrawal, P. (1984) 'Sharecropping, supervision cost, and rural credit markets', mimeographed, Department of Economics, Stanford University.

Ajami, I. (1973) 'Land reform and modernisation of the farming structure in Iran', *Oxford Agrarian Studies*, vol. 2.

—— (1975) *Shishdāngi: Pizhuhishi dar zamineh-yi jami 'ehshināsi-yi rustā'i* [Six *dangs*: an enquiry in the field of rural sociology], 4th edn, n.p.: Tus Publications.

—— (1976) 'Agrarian reform, modernization of peasants and agricultural development in Iran', in J.W. Jacqz (ed.) *Iran: Past, Present and Future*, New York: Aspen Institute for Humanistic Studies.

Alexander, R.J. (1974) *Agrarian Reform in Latin America*, New York: Macmillan.

Antoun, R.T. (1976) 'The gentry of a traditional peasant community undergoing rapid technological change: an Iranian case study', *Iranian Studies*, vol. 9.

—— (1981) 'The complexity of the lower stratum: sharecroppers and wage-labourers in an Iranian village', *Iranian Studies*, vol. 14.

Aresvik, O. (1976) *The Agricultural Development of Iran*, New York: Praeger Publishers.

Asayesh, H. (1974) 'Barrasi-yi tahlili-yi budjeh khānivārhā-yi shahri va rusta'i-yi Azarbayjan-i Shirqi' [Analysis of income and consumption of rural and urban families of East Azarbayjan], *Nashriyeh Dānishkadeh-yi Adabiyāt va 'ulumi-i Insani-yi Tabriz*, vol. 26.

Agriculture, poverty and reform in Iran

Agriculture, poverty and reform in Iran

Agriculture, poverty and reform in Iran

Agriculture, poverty and reform in Iran

Ashraf, A. (1979) 'Ābādi' [village], *Ayandeh*, vol. 5.

Ashraf, A. and Banuazizi, A. (1980) 'Policies and strategies of land reform in Iran', in Inayatullah (ed.), *Land Reform: Some Asian Experiences* vol. IV, Kuala Lumpur: Asian and Pacific Development Administration Office.

Azkia, M. (1980) 'The effect of rural development programmes on the Iranian peasantry between 1962 and 1978, with special reference to far corporations', Ph.D. Dissertation, Aberdeen University.

—— (1986) *Jāmi 'ehshinasi-yi tusi eh va tuse 'ehnayāftigi-yi rustā'i-yi Iran* [Sociology of development and rural underdevelopment of Iran], Tehran: Ettel'at Publications.

Bagley, R.F.C. (1976) 'A bright future after oil: dams and agro-industry in Khuzistan', *The Middle East Journal*, vol. 30.

Bank Markazi Iran (The Central Bank of Iran) (annually 1965–77) *Annual Report and Balance Sheet*, Tehran.

—— (1968) *Bulletin*, no. 39.

—— (1969) *National Income of Iran: 1962–67*, Tehran: Bank Melli Iran Press.

—— (1974) *National Income of Iran: 1959–72*, Tehran: Bank Melli Iran Press.

—— (1975) *Bulletin*, no. 76.

Bardhan, P.K. (1973) 'Size, productivity, and returns to scale: an analysis of farm-level data in Indian agriculture, *Journal of Political Economy*, vol. 81.

Bardhan, P.K. and Srinivasan, T.N. (1971) 'Cropsharing in agriculture: a theoretical and empirical analysis', *American Economic Review*, vol. 6.

Barlowe, R. (1953) 'Land reform and economic development, *Journal of Farm Economics*, vol. 35.

Barraclough, S. (1970) 'Alternative land tenure systems resulting from agrarian reform in Latin America', *Land Economics*, vol. 45.

Bavandi, B. (1982) 'Masā'il-i ijtima'i va rifāhi dar rustāhā-yi Iran' [Social and welfare problems in the Iranian villages], *Masā'il-i Kishāvarzi-yi Iran*, vol. 2.

Bell, C. (1976) 'Production conditions, innovation and the choice of lease in agriculture', *Sankhy: The Indian Journal of Statistics*, vol. 38.

—— (1977) 'Alternative theories of sharecropping: some tests using evidence from northeast India, *Journal of Development Studies*, vol. 13.

Bell, C. and Zusman, P. (1976) 'A bargaining theoretic approach to crop sharing contracts', *American Economic Review*, vol. 66.

Benjamin, N.C., Devarajan, S., and Weiner, R.J. (1989) 'The "Dutch" disease in a developing country: oil reserves in Cameroon', *Journal of Developing Economics*, vol. 30.

Bergamann, T. (1977) 'Agrarian reforms and their functions in development process', *Land Reform, Land Settlement, and Co-operatives*, no. 2.

Berry, R.A. (1971) 'Land reform and the agricultural income distribution', *Pakistan Development Review*, vol. 21.

Berry, R.A. and Cline, W.R. (1979) *Agrarian Structure and Productivity in Developing Countries*, Baltimore: Johns Hopkins University Press.

Bhaduri, A. (1973) 'A study in agricultural backwardness under semi-feudalism', *Economic Journal*, vol. 83.

Bharier, J. (1971) *Economic Development in Iran 1900–1970*, London: Oxford University Press.

Black, A.G. (1948) 'Iranian agriculture: present and prospective', *Journal of Farm Economics*.

Bolukbashi, A. (1981) 'Zāri', tabi'at va ravabit-i toulidi dar kishāvarzi-yi Iran' [Peasant, nature, production relations in Iranian agriculture], *Masā'il-i Kishāvarzi-yi Iran*, no. 2.

Boxley, R.F. (1971) 'Cost-share leases revisited . . . again', *American Journal of Agricultural Economics*, vol. 53.

Brun, T. and Dumont, R. (1978) 'Iran: imperial pretensions and agricultural dependence', *Merip Reports*, vol. 8.

Caballero, J.M. (1983) 'Sharecropping as an efficient system: further answers to an old puzzle', in T.J. Byres (ed.), *Sharecropping and Share-croppers*, London: Frank Cass.

Cheung, S.N.S. (1968) 'Private property rights and sharecropping', *Journal of Political Economy*, vol. 76.

—— (1969) *The Theory of Share Tenancy*, Chicago: University of Chicago Press.

Corden, W.M. and Neary, P. (1982) 'Booming sector and de-industrialisation in a small open economy', *Economic Journal*, vol. 92.

Corina, G.A. (1985) 'Farm size, land yields, and the agricultural production functions: an analysis for fifteen developing countries', *World Development*, vol. 13.

Cottam, R.W. (1964) *Nationalism in Iran*, Pittsburgh: University of Pittsburgh Press.

Craig, O. (1978) 'The impact of land reform on an Iranian village', *Middle East Journal*, vol. 33.

Dehbod, A. (1963) 'Land ownership and use in Iran', *CENTO Symposium on Rural Development*, Tehran: CENTO.

De Janvry, A. (1981) *The Agrarian Question and Reformism in Latin America*, Baltimore: Johns Hopkins University Press.

Denman, D.R. (1973) *The King's Vista: A Land Reform which has Changed the Face of Persia*, Berkhamsted: Geographical Publications.

—— (1978) 'Land reforms of Shah and people', in G. Lenczowski (ed.), *Iran Under the Pahlavis*, California: Hoover Institution Press.

Dorner, P. (1972) *Land Reform and Economic Development*, Harmondsworth: Penguin Books.

Doroudian, A. (1976) 'Modernization of rural economy in Iran', in J.W. Jacqz (ed.) *Iran: Past, Present and Future*, New York: Aspen Institute for Humanistic Studies.

Dovring, F. (1970) 'Economic results of land reform', *AID Spring Review of Land Reform*, vol. XI.

Dumont, R. (1978) *Nukāti chand dabāreh-yi vaz 'nyat-i kishāvarzi-yi Iran* [Some remarks on the situation of Iranian agriculture], Frankfurt: Confederation of Iranian Students.

Ettel'at (1980) 20 February.

—— (1986) 26 October.

FAO (annual) *Production Yearbook*, Rome: FAO.

FAO (1966) *Report on the 1960 World Census of Agriculture*, Rome: FAO.

Fishburne, C. (1964) 'The United States policy toward Iran', unpublished Ph.D. dissertation, Florida State University.

Flores, E. (1970) 'Issues of land reform', *Journal of Political Economy*, vol. 78.

Freivalds, J. (1972) 'Farm corporation in Iran: an alternative to traditional agriculture', *Middle East Journal*, vol. 24.

Ghose, A.K. (1983) 'Agrarian reform in developing countries: issues of theory and problems of practice', in A.K. Ghose (ed.) *Agrarian Reform in Contemporary Developing Countries*, London: Croom Helm.

Ghose, A. and Griffin, K. (1980) 'Rural poverty and development alternatives in south and southeast Asia: some policy issues', *Development and Change*, vol. 11.

Gittinger, J.R. (1961) 'United States policy toward agrarian reform in underdeveloped nations', *Land Economics*, vol. 37.

Griffin, K. (1974) *The Political Economy of Agrarian Change*, London: Macmillan.

—— (1976) *Land Concentration and Rural Poverty*, London: Macmillan.

Group of Experts (1980) 'Darbāreh-yi shirkathā-yi sahami-yi zirā'i va sarni-visht-i ān' [On farm corporations and their destiny], *Masā'il-i Kishavarzi-yi Iran*, no. 1.

Hadary, G. (1951) 'The agrarian reform problem in Iran', *The Middle East Journal*, vol. 5.

Hakimian, H. (1988) 'The impact of the 1970s' oil boom on Iranian agriculture', *Journal of Peasant Studies*, vol. 15.

Halliday, F. (1979) *Iran: Dictatorship and Development*, Harmondsworth: Penguin Books.

Haririan, M. (1976) 'Tahavul-i iqtisād-i rustā'i dar Dasht-i Chamchamāl' [Transformation of rural economy in Chamchal Plain], *Majaleh-yi Dānishkadeh-yi Adabiyāt va 'ulum-i Insani-yi Dānishgah-i Ferdousi*, vol. 46.

Heady, E.O. (1955) 'Marginal resource productivity and imputation of share for a sample of rented farms', *Journal of Political Economy*, vol. 63.

Ho, S.P.S. (1976) 'Uncertainty and the choice of tenure arrangements: some hypotheses', *American Journal of Agricultural Economics*, vol. 58.

Homan, A. (1955) *Iqtisād-i kishvārzi* [Agricultural economics], Tehran: Tehran University Press.

Hooglund, E. (1973) 'The Khwushninin population of Iran', *Iranian Studies*, vol. 6.

—— (1982) *Land and Revolution in Iran, 1960–1980*, Austin: University of Texas Press.

Hooglund, M. (1980) 'One village in the revolution', *MERIP Reports*, no. 87.

Hsiao, J.C. (1975) 'The theory of share tenancy revisited', *Journal of Political Economy*, vol. 83.

Huang, Y. (1973) 'Risk, entrepreneurship, and tenancy', *Journal of Political Economy*, vol. 83.

Huntington, S.P. (1970) 'Political dimensions of land reform', *AID Spring Review of Land Reform*, vol. 11.

Iran Almanac and Book of Facts (annual) Tehran: Echo of Iran.

Issawi, C. (1957) 'Farm output under fixed rents and share tenancy', *Land Economics*, vol. 33.

Jacoby, E. (1971) *Man and Land*, London: Andre Deutsch.

Jacqz, J.W. (ed.) (1976) *Iran: Past, Present and Future*, New York: Aspen Institute for Humanistic Studies.

Jaynes, G.D. (1982) 'Production and distribution in agrarian economies', *Oxford Economic Papers*, vol. 34.

Jones, R. (1967) 'The short-run economic impact of land reform on fedual village irrigated agriculture', unpublished dissertation, University of Maryland.

Johnston, B.F. and Kilby, P. (1975) *Agricultural and Structural Transformation*, London: Oxford University Press.

Johnson, D.G. (1950) 'Resource allocation under share contracts', *Journal of Political Economy*, vol. 58.

Kamali, T. (1982) 'Kisht-i birinj dar Iran' [Rice cultivation in Iran], *Masā'il Kishāvarzi-yi Iran*, no. 6.

Katouzian, H. (1983) 'The agrarian question in Iran', in A.K. Ghose (ed.) *Agrarian Reform in Contemporary Developing Countries*, London: Croom Helm.

Katouzian, M.A. (1974) 'Land reform in Iran: a case study of the political economy of social engineering, *Journal of Peasant Studies*, vol. 1.

—— (1978) 'Oil versus agriculture: a case of dual resource depletion in Iran', *Journal of Peasant Studies*, vol. 5.

Kazemi, F. (1980) *Poverty and Revolution in Iran*, New York: New York University Press.

Kazemi, F. and Abrahamian, E. (1978) 'The nonrevolutionary peasantry of modern Iran', *Iranian Studies*, vol. 11.

Keddie, N.R. (1968) 'The Iranian village before and after land reform', *Journal of Contemporary History*, vol. 3.

—— (1972) 'Stratification, social control, and capitalism in Iranian villages: before and after land reform', in R. Antoun and A.I. Harik (eds) *Rural Politics and Social Change in the Middle East*, London: Indian University Press.

Khatibi, N. (1972) 'Land reform in Iran and its role in rural development', *Land Reform, and Land Settlement and Cooperatives*, no. 1.

Khirabi, J. (1981) 'Intikhāb-i munāsib-i qanāt va ya chāh bar cheh mavāzini bāyad ustuvār bāshid?' [What should be the criteria for the proper choice of *qanat* or well?], *Masā'il-i Kishāvarzi-yi Iran*, no. 3.

Khosrovi, K. (1979a) *Jami'eh-yi dehqāni dar Iran* [Peasant society in Iran], Tehran: Payam Publications, 1978; reprint edn 1979.

—— (1979b) *Jami'ehshināsi-yi rustā'i-yi Iran* [Rural sociology of Iran], Tehran, University of Tehran 1972; reprint edn 1979, Tehran: Payam Publications.

169

—— (1981) *Mas'leh-yi arzi va dihqānañ-i tuhidast dar Iran* [Agrarian question and poor peasants in Iran], Tehran: Bidari Publication.

—— (1982) *Dihqānān-i tavāngir* [Rich peasants], Tehran: Mitra Publications.

King, R. (1977) *Land Reform: A World Survey*, Colorado: Westview Press.

Koo, A.Y.C. (1973) 'Towards a more general model of land tenancy and reform', *Quarterly Journal of Economics*, vol. 87.

Lambton, A.K.S. (1953) *Landlord and Peasant in Persia*, London: Oxford University Press.

—— (1969) *The Persian Land Reform: 1962–1966*, Oxford: Clarendon Press.

—— (1971) 'Land reform and the rural cooperative societies', in E. Yar-Shater (ed.), *Iran Faces Seventies*, New York: Praeger Publishers.

Land, C.T. (1965/6) 'Land reform in Iran', *Persica*, no. 2.

Layman, P.N. and French, J.T. (1970) 'Political results of land reform', *AID Spring Review of Land Reform*, Washingron DC: AID.

Lipton, M. (1968) 'The theory of optimizing peasant', *Journal of Development Studies*, vol. 4.

—— (1974) 'Towards a theory of land reform', in D. Lehmann (ed.), *Agrarian Reform and Agrarian Reformism*, London: Faber & Faber.

Lodi, H.S.K. (1965) 'Preharvest sale of agricultural produce in Iran', *Monthly Bulletin of Agricultural Economics and Statistics*, vol. 14.

Lucas, R.E.B. (1979) 'Sharing, monitoring, and incentives: Marshallian misallocation reassessed', *Journal of Political Economy*, vol. 87.

Lundahl, M. (1979) *Peasants and Poverty: A Study of Haiti*, London: Croom Helm.

—— (1984) 'Jord och fattigdom i Latinamerika' [Land and poverty in Latin America], *Ekonomisk debatt*, no. 8.

McLachlan, K.S. (1968) 'Land reform in Iran', in W.B. Fisher (ed.), *The Cambridge History of Iran* vol. I, Cambridge: Cambridge University Press.

—— (1977) 'The Iranian economy', in H. Amirsadeghi (ed.), *Twentieth-Century Iran*, London: Heinemann.

Mahdavy, H. (1965) 'The coming crisis in Iran', *Foreign Affairs*, vol. 44.

—— (1982) 'Tahavulāt-i sisaleh-yi yik dih dar Dasht-i Qazvin', [The 30-year changes of a village in Qazvin Plain], in Agah Book Collection, 1982.

Majd, M.G. (1987) 'Land reform policies in Iran', *American Journal of Agricultural Economics*, vol. 69.

Marshall, A. (1920) *Principles of Economics*, London: Macmillan.

Mazumdar, D. (1975) 'The theory of sharecropping with labor market dualism', *Economica*, vol. 42.

Ministry of Interior (1961) *National and Province Statistics of the First Census of Iran: November 1956*, Tehran: Ministry of Interior.

Misawa, T. (1974) 'Agricultural development and employment expansion: a case study of Japan', in N. Islam (ed.), *Agricultural Policy in Developing Countries*, London: Macmillan.

Mohammadi, M. (1973) *Darbāreh-yi mas'leh-yi arzi dar Iran va shiveh-yi hal-i dimokrātik-i ān* [On the agrarian question in Iran and its democratic solution], Stassfurt: Tudeh Publishing Center.

Momeni, B. (1980) *Mas'leh-yi arzi va jang-i tabaqāti dar Iran* [The agrarian question and class struggle in Iran], Tehran: Peyvand Publications.

Newbery, D.M.G. (1974) 'Cropshare tenancy in agriculture: comment', *American Economic Review*, vol. 64.

—— (1975a) 'Tenurial obstacles to innovation', *Journal of Development Studies*, vol. 11.

—— (1975b) 'The choice of rental contract in peasant agriculture', in L.G. Reynolds (ed.), *Agriculture in Development Theory*, New Haven: Yale University Press.

—— (1977) 'Risk sharing, sharecropping, and uncertain labor market', *Review of Economic Studies*, vol. 44.

Newbery, D.M.G. and Stiglitz, J.E. (1979) 'Sharecropping, risk sharing and the importance of imperfect information', in Roumasset, Boussard and Singh (eds), *Risk, Uncertainty and Agricultural Development*, New York: Agricultural Development Council.

Nikayin, A. (1976) 'Silsileh-yi Pahlavi, amlāk zirā'iti, dihqānān' [Pahlavi dynasty, agricultural lands, peasants], *Donya*, vol. 3.

Nomani, F. (1980) *Takāmul-i feodālism dar Iran* [Development of feudalism in Iran], Tehran: Kharazmi Publications.

OIPFG (The Organisation of Iranian People's Feddyi Guerrilla) (1973) *Darbāreh-yi islāhāt arzi va natā'ij-i mustaqim-i ān* [On the land reform in Iran and its direct results], Rural Studies Series of OIPFG, no. 1, n.p.: OIPFG Publications.

—— (1974) *Barrasi-yi sākht-i iqtisādi-yi rustāhā-yi Kirman* [A study of the economic structure of the villages of Kerman], Rural Studies Series of OIPFG, no. 4, n.p.: OIPFG Publications.

Okazaki, S. (1968) *The Development of Large-Scale Farming in Iran: The Case of Province of Gorgan*, Tokyo: Institute of Asian Economic Affairs.

Parvin, M. and Zamani, A. (1979) 'Political economy of growth and destruction: a statistical interpretation of the Iranian case', *Iranian Studies*, vol. 12.

Pertev, R. (1986) 'A new model for sharecropping and peasant holdings', *Journal of Peasants Studies*, vol. 14.

Pesaran, M.H. (1976) 'Income distribution and its major determinants in Iran', in J.W. Jacqz (ed.) *Iran: Past, Present and Future*, New York: Aspen Institute for Humanistic Studies.

Platt, K.B. (1970) 'Land reform in Iran', *AID Spring Review of Land Reform*, vol. 11.

Price, O.T.W. (1975) 'Towards a comprehensive Iranian agricultural policy', Agricultural and Rural Development Advisory Mission (ARDAMI) Report no. 1, Tehran: IBRD.

Rafipoor, F. (1985) *Jāmi'eh-yi rustā'i va niyāzhā-yi ān: Pizhuhishi dar 32 rustā-yi barguzideh-yi ustān Yazd* [Rural society and its needs: an analysis of 32 sample villages of Yazd Province], Tehran: Inteshar Corporation.

Rao, C.H.H. (1971) 'Uncertainty, entrepreneurship, and sharecropping in India', *Journal of Political Economy*, vol. 79.

Raup, P. (1968) 'Land reform and agricultural development', in Southworth and Johnston (eds), *Agricultural Development and Economic Growth*, New York: Cornell University Press.

Reid, D.J. (1976) 'Sharecropping and agricultural uncertainty', *Economic Development and Cultural Change*, vol. 24.

—— (1977) 'The theory of share tenancy revisited again', *Journal of Political Economy*, vol. 85.

Research Group (1962) 'Tarh-i tahqiq-i ghalāt dar Iran' [The research project of crop economy in Iran], *Tahqiqāt-e Eqtesadi*, nos 1 and 2.

—— (1964) 'A review of the statistics of the first stage of land reform', *Tahqiqat-e Eqtesadi*, nos 7 and 8.

—— (1965a) 'Economic report on agriculture in the Isfahan and Yazd area', *Tahqiqat-e Eqtesadi*, nos 9 and 10.

—— (1965b) 'Rural economic problems of Khuzistan, *Tahqiqāt-e Eqtesadi*, nos 9 and 10.

—— (1967) 'A study of rural economic problems of Gilan and Mazandarn', *Tahqiqat-e Eqtesadi*, no. 3.

—— (1968) 'A study of rural economic problems of East and West Azarbaijan', *Tahqiqat-e Eqtesadi*, nos 12 and 13.

—— (1970a) 'An analysis of the law governing the first stage of land reform in Iran', *Tahqiqat-e Eqtesadi*, no. 17.

—— (1970b) 'A study of the rural economic problems of Sistan and Baluchestan', *Tahqiqat-e Eqtesadi*, nos 12 and 13.

Richards, H. (1975) 'Land reform and agribusiness in Iran', *Merip Reports*, no. 43.

Saedloo, H. (1972) 'A critique of a policy for agricultural development at the poles of soil and water', *Tahqiqat-e Eqtesadi*, nos 25 and 26.

—— (1979) 'Huvaiyt-i kishāvarzi-yi Īran' [Identity of the Iranian agriculture], *Ayandeh*, vol. 5.

Saeedi, A. (1975) 'Pitzhuhishi dar Kifaiyt-i muhājirthā-yi rustā'i dar Shamāl-i Khurāsān' [An analysis of the quality of rural migration in the northern Khorasan], *Majaleh-yi Dānniskadeh-yi Adbiyat va 'Ulum-i Insani-yi Dānishgah-i Ferdousi*, vol. 44.

Safinezhad, J. (1966) *Tālibābād: Numuneh-yi jāmi'i az barrasi-yi yik dih* [Talebabad: a detailed example of the study of one village], Tehran: University of Tehran.

—— (1972) *Buneh*, Tehran: University of Tehran Press (in Persian).

Salmanzadeh, C. and Jones, G.E. (1979) 'An approach to the micro analysis of the land reform program in southwestern Iran', *Land Economics*, vol. 55.

Salour, A. (1963) 'Land reform activities in Iran', *CENTO Symposium on Rural Development*, Tehran: CENTO.

Scherr, S.J. (1989) 'Agriculture in an export-boom economy: a comparative analysis of policy and performance in Indonesia, Mexico and Nigeria', *World Development*, vol. 17.

Schickele, R. (1941) 'Effects of tenure systems on agricultural efficiency', *Journal of Farm Economics*.

Sen, A.K. (1975) *Employment, Technology and Development*, Oxford: Clarendon Press.

Siyahpoosh, T. (1981) 'Kishāvarzi-yi sunati ra bishināsim', [We should know the traditional agriculture], *Masa'il-i Kishāvarzi-yi Iran*, no. 3.

Smith, A. (1937) [1776] *Wealth of Nations*, New York: Modern Library edition.

Soodagar, M. (1978) *Nizām-i arbāb ra'iyati dar Iran* [The landlord–peasant system in Iran], Tehran: Pazand Publications.

Statistical Centre of Iran (1966) *Statistical Yearbook: 1966*, Tehran: Statistical Centre of Iran.

—— (1971) *Statistical Yearbook: 1968*, Tehran: Statistical Centre of Iran.

—— (1972) *Statistical Yearbook: 1970*, Tehran: Statistical Centre of Iran.

—— (1975) *Statistical Yearbook: 1972*, Tehran: Statistical Centre of Iran.

—— (1976) *Statistical Yearbook: 1973*, Tehran: Statistical Centre of Iran.

—— (1981) *Natā'ij-i āmargiri az budjeh-i Khānivārhā-yi rustā'i sāl-i 1356* [The results of the 1977 census of budget of rural households], Tehran: Statistical Centre of Iran.

—— (1984) *Sālnāmeh-yi amari-yi 1361* [Statistical Yearbook: 1982], Tehran: Statistical Centre of Iran.

Stenberg, M.J. (1970) 'The economic impact of the latifundista', *Land Reform, Land Settlement, and Cooperatives*, no. 2.

Stickley, S. and Najafi, B. (1971) 'The effectiveness of farm corporations in Iran', *Tahqiqat-e Eqtesadi*, nos 25 and 26.

Stiglitz, J.E. (1974) 'Incentives and risk sharing in sharecropping', *Review of Economic Studies*, vol. 41.

Taqavi, N. (1983) 'Āb va ābyari dar rustāhā-yi Iran' [Water and irrigation in the Iranian villages], *Nashryeh-yi Dānnishkadey-yi Ādabiyat va 'Ulum-i Insani*, vol. 31.

UN (1963) *Progress in Land Reform. Third Report*, New York: Department of Economic and Social Affairs.

Vreeland, H.H. (ed.) (1957) *Iran*, New Haven: Human Relations Area Files.

Walinsky, L. (ed.) (1977) *Agrarian Reform as Unfinished Business: the Selected Papers of Wolf Ladejinsky*, New York: Oxford University Press.

Warriner, D. (1969) *Land Reform in Principle and Practice*, Oxford: Clarendon Press.

Weeks, J. (1970) 'Uncertainty, risk and wealth and income distribution in peasant agriculture', *Journal of Development Studies*, vol. 7.

Wulff, H.E. (1966) *The Traditional Crafts of Persia*, Cambridge: MIT Press.

Yavari, A. (1981) *Shinākhti az Kishāvarzi-yi sunati-yi Iran* [Information on Iranian Traditional Agriculture], Tehran: Book Publication and Translation Company.

Zonis, M. (1971) *The Political Elite of Iran*, Princeton: Princeton University Press.

Index

absentee landowners 9, 25–6,
  30–1, 41, 104
agrarian reform *see* land reform
agrarian system: *arab-raiyati*
  system in Iran 28–48; bimodal
  54–61, 66–7, 77, 78, 110–11,
  143–4; traditional 8; unimodal
  61–6, 67, 77, 143
agribusinesses 83, 107, 113, 123;
  imported machinery exempt
  from taxes 123
Agricultural Bank (Agricultural
  Co-operative Bank of Iran)
  114–15, 116–17
Agricultural Development Bank of
  Iran 114, 117
Agricultural Development Fund
  84
agricultural growth: as a result of
  land reform 1; statistics 132–3
agricultural production 42–3, 83
agriculture: in Iran 4–7; techniques
  of production 40–2; *see also*
  farming
Amini, Ali 82
amlak 32
Arsanjani, Hassan 82–3

bank loans 114–17
Bank Markazi Iran 3
Bardhan, P.K. 13, 17
barley 7, 125, 129, 130; yield 42
barzigars 38
beet 130
Bell, C. 14, 15, 18

bimodal agrarian system 54–61,
  66–7, 77, 78, 110–11, 143–4
Black, A.G. 31
Boxley, R.F. 14
bread price 130, 131
buneh 37–8, 103

Caballero, J.M. 15
cash crops 59–60, 61, 111, 125–9,
  130
Central Bank *see* Bank Markazi
  Iran
Cereals Organization 131
Cheung, S.N.S. 12–13, 15, 17, 21,
  24
co-operative societies 85–6,
  114–19
co-operatives (*buneh*) 37–8
conservation of water 42
contracts *see* tenancy contracts
corporations, farm 84, 107–8,
  113, 123, 141; privileges 118
corruption 69
cotton 129, 130
credit 45, 64, 85; scarcity 130; *see
  also* loans
crops: division in a shared tenancy
  38–9; food 60, 61, 125–6, 129;
  pre-harvest sale 45, 46–7; staple
  7; subsistence 111; summer 7;
  see also cash crops

Denman, D.R. 101

economics of land reform 53–66

174